THE UNRESTRICTABLE YOU

A COLLECTION OF ENCOURAGING THOUGHTS AND INSPIRATIONAL JUMP STARTS

KC O'KERRY

CONTENTS

SECTION I
MOTIVATIONAL MESSAGES

There are moments we find ourselves vulnerable to situations and circumstances that are beyond our control. These are moments of despair, frustration, and trepidation. We throw our hands up in the air and say it's all over. But just at our breaking point, we hear a word of encouragement, some advice that touches the very core of our challenge, a word that reaches the very depth of our soul and awakens us to possibilities. Such is the power of words to motivate. This article has many transformative words that will cause you to rise from hopelessness to reach your true state of being-ness.

THE AWAKENING

I used to be spineless. If there was a definition of the word "coward," I was the totality of whatever it means. I feared everything, from my past to the future. I feared people, I feared objects, I feared everything and anything, and from early childhood, I knew fear.

As a child, I noticed these tendencies and I didn't like them, so one day I said to myself that I was going to break free. I can still remember vividly that Tuesday afternoon. I was in grade 7, and there was a student who had terrorized my life since my first day at school. Each day, as I made plans to go to school, I ensured that my escape routes were clearly laid out, in case the need arose. But this day, I made up my mind that I was going to put an end to my fears, I was going to confront my adversary and use the experience to break free from all other fear bondages. So, I walked up to my bully and told him boldly to meet me at the back of the school building after school … alone.

I knew I was no match for him in a fight, I did not have any fighting skills or experience, in fact, I had never fought with anyone before. He was bigger and looked much stronger compared to my frail four-foot height. I knew I was going to get the beating of my life, but a man's got to do what he's got to do. So, like a sheep being led to the slaughter, my reluctant feet dragged my frail little body to meet with my adversary. On our way to the fight, my best friend tried to dissuade me, but I faked bravery as I brushed him aside with a flourish and walked with the strongest stride a 12 year-old could muster. As we arrived at a small clearing, my assailant wasted no time in the business of the day as he launched his first blow. It caught me on my left eye, and before I could recover from that, I felt two other punches almost simultaneously on my chest and head; he was ferocious, launching blow after blow like some raging lunatic with the consistency of a journeyman carpenter from Fort McMurray – he was a fighting demon. Suddenly my instincts kicked in, and I knew exactly what to do … I fled.

That is the way it was … I was a runner. I ran away from every battle, whether seen or only perceived. What a life, what a cowardly life I lived. Now, when I look back, I say to myself, I wish I had demonstrated at least one act of bravery, one little effort to prove I had some backbone, but alas, I did nothing (except for confronting that bully at school). I lived my entire life without standing my ground. I have been tossed about by everyone and everything – the young, the old, the big, the small, the fat, the thin, the weak, the strong. Sometimes I felt like a punching bag that anyone can have a swing at, anytime, anywhere. I would shake my head and wonder how much worse it could get. Because I did not want to hurt people's feelings, I became their doormat. I was a tool in everybody's hand, what a life.

As I got older, the urge to break free became stronger; I knew there had to be an end to this way of living, there had to be an end to being pushed around, there must be a way to stop this cowardice. Somehow, I knew the answer to this problem was in my hands, but I didn't know how to fix it.

Then one day, I died. I died to my feelings and what people

thought about me; I died to political correctness and religious piety; I died to shame, vulnerability, and devotedness; I died to the urge to please everybody at my own expense; I died to everything that represented my negative past, my present, and my future. I died to myself.

Then I woke. I woke to realise that my world was under my control. That I didn't have to be scared of anyone or cater to everybody's needs. Suddenly, I realized my feeling of weakness was only an illusion and that my conscious mind was deliberately sabotaging my efforts by feeding me with wrong perceptions. My conscious mind was telling me that I was weak when I was strong, it was telling me to run when there was nothing to fear, it was telling me to quit when the obstacle before me was just a tiny obstruction; my conscious mind was fooling me and I didn't know it, I bought all the lies, hook, line, and sinker.

Many a time we see the world through tinted lenses. These tints or filters are synonymous with our feelings, because the feeling we apply to whatever we perceive determines our reaction. If we perceive fear, we want to run; if it's anger, we brace ourselves for the onslaught; if it's verbal abuse, we recoil or we build up our defence mechanism. But what if we remove these filters; wouldn't the world look different and feel different? When a stranger smiles at you, will you be brave enough to smile back or will you be suspicious of his intentions? What are *your* perceptual filters? Isn't this perceptual filter the reason that the world appears the way it does today? Is it really difficult to love or trust one another? I know many people who have been hurt when they opened themselves up to love, including me, but should that make us throw loving one another out the window? Isn't it easier to love than to hate? Can't we just live in the moment and savour the joy, the kindness, and the beauty we share, and just relish its wonderful enfoldment?

Anger, hate, and negative emotions have powerful impacts on our lives. Dr Joe Dispenza explained the process we use to inflict disease upon ourselves through the power of thought. He said that every time we have a thought, we make chemicals that send signals through the body to make it feel what we were just thinking. He said, once we start feeling negative, our feelings make our thoughts more negative which, in turn, activates more chemicals that cause our body to mirror our negative thoughts, creating a vicious cycle and a negative state of being. The thought we hold in our consciousness translates to our life experience.

It is for our own good, therefore, to not hold contrary opinions of people or of ourselves, or of any situation. All circumstances and all people are good, irrespective of the conditions surrounding them. Look positively on whatever circumstance you find yourself in; positive thinking is an exceptional tool that douses all kinds of negative situations; it breeds harmony and causes you to find favour among men. Hold thoughts of perfection and possibilities at all times. It is a law that the thought you hold in your consciousness will be manifested, irrespective of situation or circumstance. In holding a good thought, you sow seeds of love and goodness. The Sanskrit reminds us that you only keep what you give away. When we spread love, joy, kindness, and goodness, we receive them in return – for what you give, you receive.

The pictures you paint in your mind become your reality. Man is first mental, then physical. Mental powers have no physical limitations. Every human is equipped with this metaphysical potential; "we can do all things,"[1] say the scriptures. The mind rules the body; the body is subject to the mind. The mind is the seat of control for all your activities. So, if you take hold of your mind, you are also taking hold of all the circumstances that surround you. And that was just what I did in combating my fears. I took hold of my mind and subjected it to the influence of the superconscious and my freedom ensued.

You too, my friend, can turn your situation around. You

don't have to sit and bemoan your fate, get up and do something. There is a dynamic force within you, there is a power within you, there is something within you telling you to rebel against the status quo, it's telling you to rebel against the circumstance holding you back, it's telling you to stand your ground and fight the fight of faith. It's time to leave mediocrity behind and stand up for what you believe. You have been pushed around for too long; it's time to wake up to your new reality of possibilities.

Ignore those small voices telling you to remain just as you are. Get up and make some real changes. It's time to feel the fresh breeze of freedom on your face, it's time to rise above every challenge of the mind, it's time to discover the power of surrendering and letting the superconscious take over. You were born free, so liberate your mind from fear and bind yourself with all power that is. Your freedom lies within your bosom; so, wake up to your true reality.

There is an African proverb that says a stranger cannot dip his hand in the oil palm soup unless the owner of the home lets him; no man has the right to subject another to bondage unless permitted to do so. You gave permission to your aggressors, you gave permission to your persecutors, and you gave permission for your captivity. It is time to reset your mindset and take control of your life.

What do you want out of life? Where do you want to be? What do you want to do? All these questions have answers that are within you. Man is a manifestation of the infinite, for we are not just mere mortals. Our lives are subject to our control. We have the ability, we have the power, we have the capacity and the authority to run our lives just as we have been destined to. There's no need to live in fear as I had lived in time past, you've got to let your mind die to your fears and live the life of the divine. The infinite dwells within you, you and the infinite are one, so "fear not, for I am with you,"[2] says the Almighty. In the scriptures we read that "He will never leave nor forsake you,"[3] You are a dynamic life force, impregnable and unlimited. You are a part of the vital force that created the universe, you are one with the infinite, and no one, and I mean no one, can mess with you. So, wake up to the reality of your true self. For you, nothing is impossible.

Life is not as complex as we perceive it to be, our negative experiences are only symphonies of our own orchestration, largely influenced by our perception which is often incorrect. All things are subject to our control, so take the reins of your life and be in charge, you are already a winner.

UNLEASHING THE POWER OF THOUGHT

$\mathcal{A}$ man's success in life is largely determined by the thoughts he thinks. His success or failure in any endeavor is long established before it is experienced or manifested. Thoughts create life experiences, your thoughts made you who you are today. Now, if thought is so important, why don't people pay attention to their thoughts? Why are people complacent about the effects of thought? It's simply because people don't understand the direct correlation between thoughts and their daily life experiences.

Thoughts control every aspect of man's affairs. Your dreams and aspirations are the seeds of your thought. Decisions regarding future endeavors are determined by your thoughts. For instance, in a LinkedIn survey of 8,000 professionals on November 15, 2012, only 30.3% of global workers said they earn a living from their childhood dream job or in a related field. These dreams and aspirations that were nurtured over time were changed in an instant of thought. You, my friend, are probably part of the 69.7% who backed out of their dreams. Why did you change your mind? Why did you give up? Do you think about your dreams sometimes and wonder how it would be now if you had persisted?

People give up on their dreams for several reasons—some quite genuine and others just excuses. But one thing I do know is that a strong desire knows no restriction. The switching on and off of your dreams, your goals and aspirations, is a function of your thought. Your failure or lack of success today is a function of your indecision powered by your thought; your current physical state is the reflection of your thought, your thoughts control every aspect of your existence, your thoughts create your current life experience, your thoughts made you who you are today.

The ability to focus thought creates a platform for future endeavors. Within your thought you determine the possibilities of any venture. When you say yes to yourself, you are saying yes to possibilities, and in order to say yes, there must be a conviction, and conviction does not come from scattered thoughts it comes from a focused mind. In his book *The Master Key System*, Charles Haanel said, "every success is being accomplished by persistent concentration upon the object in view." Please note the words "persistent concentration." Whatsoever you set your mind on; if you stay focused it definitely comes to light. Charles Haanel also said, "The ideal steadily held in mind is what predetermines and attracts the necessary conditions for its fulfilment." The secret of every success lies in harnessing the power of thought; you must be focused at all times to create the experience you specifically desire. When you have too many kettles on the fire you are scattering your forces, you can never get that water boiling!

Time and again, we've heard messages reminding us about the power of thought, and every religion has something to say about this, yet the meaning seem to elude us. The book of Proverbs 4:23 says "keep thy heart with all diligence for out of it are the issues of life." The mind is everything, what you think, you become. Be careful with what you think about. Thought is the most powerful tool in the hands of man. Thought takes precedence over words and action.

Rene Descartes, the renowned French philosopher and mathematician, once said, "I think, therefore I am." You cannot be alienated from your thought, you are what you think, you are a reflection of your thoughts, you are your own creation, and as the Bible says "ye are gods.[1]" We all are creators, constantly making manifestations of the thoughts we hold in our consciousness. Everything you see, touch, and smell made by man originated from thought, from the great architectural structures to nanotechnologies, they all originate from ideas or thought.

What are your goals? What are your dreams? What are your aspirations? How determined are you to see these dreams come to life? Many set out with lofty ideas but after a while experience doubt. Doubt is a type of thought; however, it is negative thought. Rae Zander, in her online radio program *Everyday Attraction* said "Doubt originates when you tell stories about your past failures or your uncertainties." The more you talk about your failures, limitations, or inadequacies, the less you believe in yourself. Doubt has only one strength, and that is the ability to make you shift your focus. The moment you shift your focus, other similar doubting thoughts follow, and in a short while you lose confidence in your abilities.

Doubt means you have focused your thought on the opposite of how your inner self feels about the subject. Rae Zander featured an extract from a workshop by Esther Hicks in the *Teachings of Abraham* in which Esther said that "it's the contradiction of energy that results in doubt", in other words, the God within is saying this is possible because I know what I am telling you right now, this is the truth, take it from me, believe me! But your mind is in doubt, your mind is considering the what ifs?

the buts, the hows? and the when? These questions form the bases of doubt!

Doubt is a major factor or reason why people give up on their dreams. They doubt their abilities, they try to work out the overall picture before they get started, and in so doing they see weak links in a plan that is yet to see the light of day. I am not saying you don't have to do your due diligence or research your idea; I am saying that once you have done this the core idea is worth a shot, trust it and execute it. Some of the challenges you see now might not arise when you get going. Your trust and alignment with source energy – God – is crucial in the activation and execution of your plan. God was around long before you came into the picture, he already knows what's ahead, let go and trust his guidance!

At the time you conceived the initial idea you were excited and enthusiastic because you were connected with divine energy or the superconscious or God. Each one of us is equipped with this connectivity, it comes with us naturally, and time and again we tune in to this source consciously or unconsciously. Your conviction of the success of your endeavor came because it was a direct inspiration from source energy, God. You had a connection at the point where you conceived the idea, it was pure and it was the truth, it came to you as is and it was clear. It is the factual presentation of truth, that was why you were excited, because you were convinced, you had a knowing, you had an understanding that this idea is worth trying!

The Bible talked about Jesus saying that we must be like children in order to enter the kingdom of God[2]. The kingdom is the realm of right ideas. Your connection with the infinite brought you to this place of destiny, that dream job, that business, that idea, they all came from a source that is infallible!. Being like a child gives you the ability to trust without questioning source energy – God. Take that impression, that initial idea as is, believe in it and believe in yourself. There are no limitations in the potentials of the human mind, you can be what you will to be, don't shift your focus, don't doubt your ideas or try to work out the end result before you get started, The answer to every question lies within that question. Every need that comes to your consciousness knows that you are the solution. The world is looking for problem solvers; you could be what we have been waiting for. Earl Nightingale in his famous speech *"The Strangest Secret"* said, "success is anyone who is realizing a worthy predetermined ideal" – note the word "predetermined." A "predetermined ideal" is a prefixed idea, a focused idea, a goal. Isaiah 50: 7 says "therefore I have set my face like a flint." A flint is a hard piece of rock. My mind is made up like a hard piece of rock, it is unchangeable because I am set on a course I must follow, and I am going nowhere until I see this dream come true!

When you experience failure in your dreams or aspirations, it's not that the infinite has failed you, oh no, you cannot fail because the infinite dwells within you, he supported you throughout the incubation period of your idea, but when you took your focus from your goals and lost the conviction that you are supported by the infinite, your thoughts misled you into thinking that you cannot succeed, and as you know, whatsoever you believe becomes your reality; that was when things started going down!

The conscious mind sees life as it is and impresses the subconscious mind with its observations and the subconscious mind never questions the conscious mind. So, the apprehensions, fears, and negative emotions the conscious mind is observing overwhelm the subconscious mind, thus filling you with fear and doubt. The more you focus on the things you see or imagine the more of those things you'll get, or the more real they'll become. Therefore, if you see your failure that is exactly what you'll get, because you are expecting it! But if you conceive the picture of success in your mind, making it as vivid as possible, and you remain focused on this one goal, nothing can stop you from attaining your dreams. You will swim over chasms of doubt and fear. Thus success will manifest in all your endeavors. Remember, a focused mind is a reality creating mind – anything is possible.

How do you hold dreams and aspirations in your mind in the midst of all these fears, confusions, and doubts?

First, conceive the idea and make it as detailed as possible, then visualize it, see and feel yourself enjoying and experiencing what you have been nurturing in your mind, and finally affirm. Affirmation is calling forth that which you have conceived in your mind. Affirmations are not some cleverly constructed words; they are audible versions of what you desire. Your choice of words is crucial in defining the end results, and if you hold on to your affirmation for at least 30 days, you'll start feeling confident, and confidence leads to belief, and belief in no time becomes faith, eventually your real life experience manifests. It is your ability to hold on that leads to manifestation, be it health, wealth, job, love, anything. This is the process of impressing your subconscious mind, ridding it of negative impressions or beliefs that the conscious mind has deposited.

You must understand that it is only you who has control over your destiny, it is only you who can turn your situation around, and it is only you who holds the keys to your success, nobody else. This life is yours for taking; the only limitations are the limitations you set for yourself. Nothing is impossible; you are your own limitation. You owe yourself the responsibility to make your future great. You can't blame anyone for your misfortune because there is no one to blame! Take a look at the sky; can you see how wide it is? The birds flying up there don't collide with one another, so it is with you; this world is so big and wide that there are limitless opportunities for everyone. Life is just one experience. It's not some kind of examination where you have a second chance to rewrite when you fail. You only come this way once, there is no second chance, and you've got to use this opportunity judiciously. You have never been here before and this opportunity is never going to repeat itself, you owe it to yourself to give life your best shot.

You owe yourself this opportunity, this privilege, this one chance. You came here because you wanted this experience. Think about it, how eager you were among the million spermatozoa your father seeded into your mother's womb, you were the fastest, the strongest, the toughest, you fought for the position to be given this one chance, this opportunity to experience life. Now look at you, do you think you have justified this precious and effortful sought after position? Every day you are creating your life experiences through the thoughts you hold in your consciousness. The level of life you live right now has always been in your head, you can never be what you have not imagined. There is so much in abundance for everyone, why live in mediocrity when the top position is open to all.

Through our thoughts and selected choices we have positioned our lives and fixed ourselves into places we have chosen. I have seen intelligent young men and women, some with university degrees – doctors, engineers, professors – all compromising, losing the vision, the goals and aspirations they once had; now they live way below their dreams and when you ask them "hey, what's going on with your life?" they'll say "you know, all fingers are not equal." Ha! Did I hear you right? Did you just say all fingers are not equal? How dare you say that, these are the kind of words that have enslaved humanity since the beginning of time. I don't care what you think or believe, I don't care if there are classes, segmentations, or segregations, as far as I am concerned, all men are born equal. I don't care what the media is telling you, I don't care what your culture dictates; I don't even care what you believe because I know one thing, that all men are born equal! There is a higher consciousness inside every one of us, no one is destined to be a failure, because

15

I know that you are more than just a Man, you are Divinity in manifestation, in other words, you have the dynamic ability to cause positive changes in your life. You are infallible!

Have you ever seen a child coming out of a woman's womb already dressed in pants, shirt, and shoes? noooooooo! Even the royals don't come into the world with crowns on their heads! We all came here same way, butt naked! You are more than who you think you are! What you become depends on you. You can be who you really want to be. What are your dreams? What are your goals? What are your aspirations? Anything is possible, be it health, wealth, or beauty, nothing is impossible to the dreamer, for with God all things are possible! And ye are gods!

Friends, it's time to give yourself a talking to, the blame game is over, nobody is responsible for your failure, you are responsible for what you are and where you are at this point in time, your thoughts have made you who you are, and right now, right here, you can change your world by changing the way you think.

In bringing this message to a close, don't forget that thought attracts thought. A pattern of thought consistently maintained will generate similar thought patterns. A thought focused on any subject after a while manifests into a life experience. Thought of abundance will generate more abundance in your life. The rich man sees wealth hence he is rich, but the poor man sees and holds poverty in his thought and so remains poor. It is very important therefore to pay keen attention to the type of thoughts you entertain. God told Abraham, "as far as you can see, I'll give unto you"[3] Only you can determine the extent to which your goals will be attained in life. How far can you see? How far do you want to go?

You may ask, "How can I keep track of my thoughts, now that I know that my thought is responsible for my predicament?" Esther and Jerry Hicks provided advice on this matter in their book *Emotional Guidance System*. They said we should consistently hold and entertain good thoughts. Any thought that makes us feel good is good thought and when we feel negative emotions in the midst of our thinking, it is definitely bad thought; that is, if a thought feels good it's in agreement with source energy – God. God is our higher consciousness or higher self, and this higher self-dwells within us. God is not an external force, you and God are one and the same, the only difference is in the degree of consciousness. So whenever you are in a train of thought that makes you uncomfortable, angry, or sad, or you feel any of the many negative emotions, source energy or God is saying "I am not a part of this, please back off!"

Saint Paul recommended in Philippian 4:8, "Finally, brethren, whatsoever things are true, whatsoever things are honest, whatsoever things are just, whatsoever things are pure, whatsoever things are lovely, whatsoever things are of good report; if there be any virtue, and if there be any praise, think on these things." Thoughts that make you progressive feel good. That explains why you were excited when you had your initial idea and source energy said there goes my child!! I believe in you! Go on, pursue your dream! I am with you, do it! do it!

So that dream, that idea that you were excited about, God, source energy, the superconscious, or whatever name you want to call the absolute, was in total agreement with you, and because the idea was divinely supported, it can never go wrong, so don't give it up. There's room for you, you can make it and be who you really want to be, nothing is too big or grandiose. This is not the time to worry about who, what, where, or when it's going to be done, it's not your responsibility to worry about the details, your only task is to make yourself available and say "yes, I am ready to run with my dream." So stay focused, sit back, relax, and watch the infinite reel out your joyous expectation in real time.

Finally, my friends, I'll leave you with the words of Marcus Aurelius, the Roman emperor: "… man's life consists of what his thoughts make of it." Also, Henry Ford, the great American industrialist said "… if you say you can or you can't you are both correct." You are what you think you are, therefore you can be what you want to be. Hold on to your positive expectations, don't turn around or falter. Be persistent and believe in yourself. Believe in your dreams and, in time, everything will come to be just as you want it to be, because … you are unrestrictable!

A QUESTION FOR THE PROCRASTINATOR: IF NOT NOW, THEN WHEN?

$\mathcal{O}$h, there you go again, choosing the less appealing option. It's been this way since childhood. In high school you couldn't get that pretty girl you admired, instead you dated her best friend. You wanted to be a medical doctor but you ended up a janitor. You wanted a five bedroom bungalow but could only afford a shared apartment. Life seems to be dealing you hard blows, but somehow you've learned to roll along. You don't seem to be disturbed living less than your full potential. Is this some sort of strategy, hoping that someday things will get better? Do you have a plan B? Because what I see doesn't look much like a plan to me.

Some time ago, I was just like you, always falling short of my expectations, but then one day I woke up. I woke up to a reality that if a change was ever going to happen, that change would have to start with me. Now, I was late in starting, but of course I did start and I made a huge difference in my life. Therefore, it's up to you, my friend. Do you really want to change those negative patterns in your life? Do you really want to live up to your full potential? Do you really want to live your best life and affirm a big yes to your dreams, hopes, and aspirations? Then this is your moment, this is your chance, this is your opportunity to be, to do, and to have all that you ever wanted in life; but are you ready? Are you ready to push back memories, memories of past errors and self-limiting beliefs? Are you ready to take a stand with the "I" that dwells within you and affirm a big yes to your best future? Are you ready to walk an extra mile to create opportunities that will transform your negative conditions into a reality of possibilities?

Please tell me, are you really going to sit still and watch life go by and assume it's okay to live just the way you are? Are you going to sit still while others take advantage of all the available opportunities while you stand aside and watch? It's time to wake up; you can be much more than who you are at the moment. Don't buy the ideas that you have limitations, that you lack skills, that you are not smart enough. You are supernatural; there is a divine essence in you that you call the "I". You've got to see life through the eyes of the divine mind. The infinite spirit is the originator of all your desires and aspirations, and he knows exactly how you can attain them. But the big question is, are you ready? Are you willing and ready to press on with those ideas that are bubbling in your head, those gifts and talents that the infinite has deposited within you? Where you are right now is based on your mindset, and you can achieve only what you conceive in your mind. Therefore, you need to examine your mind, you need to know why you are sabotaging your future and setting up mental barriers that are crippling your progress. I know you can do better and that this very moment is your best chance to make a change in your life. But, are you ready to block out your past and unveil the new you? Are you ready to challenge the status quo and determined to make a positive change? Do not let this moment pass by, my friend, this is your moment, your best opportunity to redefine your future. But if you think I am wrong, then tell me, because if not now, then when?

You procrastinate. Time and again you move things you should have done yesterday to dates unknown. Day after day you sit and stare, watching your youth fade away; your dreams and aspirations have been discarded like some filthy rag. In your soliloquy I have heard you say "what have I done with my life?" I wonder, too! Did you really try your best? Did you put in your very best effort? Did you push hard enough at those dreams, those goals, those aspirations? When will you put those ideas to work? Don't tell me there is still time, because you are not getting younger. Time flies, morning becomes evening, days become weeks, months become years. Do you still want to put off what you can do today until another day? I don't think it's a good idea to miss this opportunity, but if you think otherwise then you tell me when; if not now, then when?

Life is a limited time opportunity. We are like little children playing musical chairs; some of us never grab a chair and sit on it when the music stops. We watch opportunities swing our way day after day but never grab an opportunity and tie it down. There is a time to work and a time to play, a time to get married and a time to have kids, a time to get an education and a time to fine tune a skill, a time to explore the world and a time to watch the world go by. There are things that can be achieved only in youth, while other undertakings need the wisdom of age; every moment gives a chance to achieve something, yet you just sit and stare. When are you going to get started?

You know you've got talent, and you've told yourself time and again that this talent can be your pathway to fame and success. You have been honing your skills for the past 15 years and hoping that someday you will have a big break. To some extent, you have had some success, because everyone in your little town knows your name and you are popular. But who needs to be a village champion when the world is out there waiting to be conquered? I perceive you have a vision of world dominance, hoping that someday you will be a huge success; but temporarily you are holding down this day job to support yourself while nurturing your big dream. You know this nine-to-five job isn't where you want to be, yet you seem to be relaxed, not really pushing yourself hard enough to get better at that thing you really love to do. Your delay is beginning to take a toll on you and I can see you are gradually losing steam. You have stopped talking about your aspirations, and the other day I saw you putting away that masterpiece you created. I know you are hurting, knowing that you are dying slowly on the inside, but some part of you still yearns for that part of you that still wants to succeed. But you hesitate. I don't see that fire in your eyes any more. I know it's not that you don't want to pursue your dreams; it's because you have gotten used to procrastinating. It's a habit that is now your way of life. Tell me when you will put to work those awesome ideas that you nourished lovingly for these many years. Can't you see how fast time is ebbing away? You are in the right moment, there's no better time than now, so go on, do it. Are you still wondering if this is the right moment? If not now, then when?

If in time past you were successful, but now because of some circumstance you can't seem to replicate your previous success, you might have reached a crossroad. Life brings us to a crossroad occasionally, a crossroad that can present opportunity or misfortune, depending on which way you turn. The choice of which direction to take is yours. I know where you are now can't be compared to where you have been, therefore, often you think it's over, but how did you come to believe that? What did you have before you got started? Nothing! Out of nothing you built a magnificent career, you became something. Only you can determine where you want to be and who you want to be. The world is full of discouraged and failed people, but there are people who failed but got back on their feet. The choice to be successful or to be a failure is all in your mind. If you were successful before you can be successful again. It doesn't matter how many times you failed, it doesn't matter how many disappointments have crossed your path, it doesn't matter what caused your downfall. Only one thing matters, that is getting back on your feet again. You still have a chance, you still have the spark. You still have the strength that got you started in the first place. So, don't let the voices of discouragement overwhelm you, stand upright and do the things you really love to do. The world needs your talent, the world needs your special skills, the world needs your expertise. This is the best moment to be alive. We have computers that can help us achieve phenomenally, we have cell phones that can put you in touch with people in split seconds, we have advanced technologies; what else do you need? This is the age of winners and everyone can be a winner. This is why I say that this is your best moment, this is your time. If you are still in doubt, tell me when is the best time to put yourself out there again. If not now, then when?

Never ever give up on your dreams. Irrespective of whatever circumstance you are going through, the challenges you face at this moment are the backbone of your future successes. It doesn't matter if you have been thrown in jail for a crime you never committed, it doesn't matter if you became pregnant as a teen, it doesn't matter if you lost both your parents and have no one to support you; in whatever situation you find yourself, you can still make a difference. There are self-made millionaires even in so-called third world countries. Opportunities lie everywhere, but people lack the willpower to bring changes to their situations. Don't let what you see, feel, or think discourage you. There are no limitations to your potentials, because behind every challenge is the unfolding of a bigger opportunity. Who said you can't get back on your feet again? Who said limitations are permanent sentences? Who said you can't turn your circumstances around? Every limiting experience is a pivot for the next attainment. Time and again we have seen people rise above challenges. The first Harley Davidson motorbike could not climb uphill. Sony Corporation's first invention was a rice cooker, but it couldn't cook rice. Harland David Sanders of Kentucky Fried Chicken had his recipe rejected 1,009 times before a restaurant accepted it. Do you want to hear more? Michael Jordan could not make the basketball team in high school, but by the end of his career he was a six times NBA champion with the Chicago Bulls. The same goes for you right now, my friend! The joke is on you! You are a bundle of infinite creativity waiting to unravel, you've got the skills, the talent, and the potential to be the best that can ever be. This is your moment that history will be made. Don't just sit there and stare, rise up and be the best that you are, because if not now, then when?

The mind is a terrible thing to waste; a talent not put to use is no good to you or to the world. Daily, the world loses the valuable talents of individuals who have refused to wake up to their realities. Do you know who you are? Do you know what the human race is all about? Do you know the limitlessness of the potential of the human mind? Man is first a spirit before he is flesh, and the spirit is not subject to human conditions and limitations. You are mind first, before you are a body, you can create your world in the mental state and bring it to the physical state. The world is waiting for you to showcase your brilliance, don't hold yourself back; your ideas, your talent, your skills are relevant and people need to see and experience your creativity. Hiding that beautiful voice or that scientific mind and all those amazing talents of yours is of no use to you or to the world. You can make a difference, and everything you need to bring that reality to pass is in your hands. So when are you going to put to work those amazing gifts of yours? Your time for procrastination is almost over. There isn't much time left, therefore this window is the moment you have been waiting for. Are you ready or not ready, because if not now, then when?

Dreams are the wings of the mind. Dream big, let your mind

soar to heights unimaginable and bring those dreams to reality by acting on them. Circumstances can't define who you are, for even in the midst of total catastrophe the dreamer can still make his dreams come true. I knew an immigrant who worked in a retail store. He was earning a minimum wage that obviously was not enough for his young family. But this man was ever so joyful, and hopeful. He had the brightest smile in the store and always looked cheerful. You could often hear him humming a tune under his breath, sometimes you would hear him sing out loud in the parking lot while doing his job. He radiated happiness. People often marveled at his joyous optimism, but no one knew that behind this smiling face was a man who had resolved to get over a painful condition of disappointment and hopelessness. In spite of his condition, he never stopped dreaming; he had his eyes set on a goal and he was determined to get there, irrespective of impediments. He was previously a senior advertising executive who couldn't find a job in his field, so he took a job in a retail store. He could have worn a sour face and sulked at every customer but he didn't, instead, he was positive in his approach to all his tasks. Therefore, customers naturally gravitated toward him, he was their favorite helper. His friendliness drew customers to chat with him, and they soon found out that he was well educated but could not find a job in his field. They started advising him on how best to get back on his feet. Soon, references, addresses, and employment offers ensued. In a short while he was out of the store. Today, that young man is the one speaking to you right now. My friends, even in my hopeless condition, I held on to my dream, and when my chance came I took it without hesitation. So, what are you doing about your situation? Will you take your chance when you see it? Are you ready for a change? Don't hesitate, if not now, then when?

Man is master of his circumstance, he creates his life experience by the thoughts he holds in his consciousness. Where you stand right now was the choice you made a long time ago. It was your choice! You can choose again and again! It's never too late to start all over. There is never a right or perfect time. The only perfect moment is the time you say "Yes, I can!" Don't let anyone fool you about being too old or too young. What you should ask yourself is, "What do I have to offer the world? Is it relevant? Will it help or improve humanity? Is it beneficial to all?" Those who discourage others with the age factor are failures themselves. What they could not achieve they try to stop others from achieving, don't listen to them. Time will prove them wrong if this is your destiny. Focus on your dream, focus on your goal, focus on your aspiration. The fact that you are now ready means this is the perfect moment, the moment where opportunity collides with your destiny. You have the skill and the relevant experience that is applicable to the task, and that is all that is required. It is never too late and it will never be too late to start. It is only you who can determine when, where, and how. The world is full of discouraged and failed people, but those who take the bull by the horns when their opportunity shows up have a success story to tell. Peter Roget, for instance, published the Thesaurus when he was 73; Harland Sanders founded KFC at 62; Ronald Reagan became a U.S. president at 69; Michael Jackson debuted on the professional music scene when he was six years old. It doesn't matter when you start, what matters is that you start. Don't let this opportunity pass you by. Write down what you have in your head, the world is eager to celebrate you. You're the best that has ever been and there's never going to be anyone like you! How will you know if you will succeed if you don't try? How will people hear or see it if you don't create it. Everyday new inventions are surfacing and each one is unique. Yours can be the next big thing the world is waiting to see! Don't ever underestimate your potential, don't think your ideas are unworthy, and don't listen when people tell you you can't make it. Within you is the power to create worlds and with you nothing is impossible. This is your chance, this is your opportunity, this is your moment, so don't hold back, your best is about to happen. If you doubt this then tell me when, because if not now, then when?

Don't sit back and watch life throw whatever it likes at you. I know at the moment you feel vulnerable. You are probably an immigrant father who had to sacrifice a lucrative career back in your home country just to be here so your kids would get a better education. You over there, you are probably a very successful career woman, currently a stay at home mother, or maybe you lost your job recently and you are wondering where to turn next. Whatever circumstance you find yourself in right now is irrelevant; what is most important is your determination to carry on, to make a difference, to fight for your ideas, your goals, your dreams, your aspirations, and to ensure they become manifest. It is time to put past humiliating experiences behind you.

I know the way you live now is not comparable to the way you lived before. However, your better future can only happen when you leave the past behind and decide to do something positive about the present. Therefore, now is your best moment and within this now is the opportunity to change, and only you can make this change happen. "Fate" is the excuse of the feeble minded. Don't settle for second best because you are the real deal, you are a diamond in the rough. Being an immigrant does not make you any less an achiever; you can still make it happen. You may have told yourself that it's over with you, and that you are just hanging on to see your kids through school. But I've got a question for you. If you ever become successful doing what you have always wanted to do, don't you think your kids will have a much better chance of success in life? Dreams know no boundaries; what can happen in one country can be replicated in any country. Don't give up on your dreams, roll up your sleeves and get to work! Quit complaining about your present life or your missed opportunities. No one has had it easy, everyone has at least one ugly story to tell, but those who ignore their negative experiences can make history. So, brace up, my friend, you are not alone in this fight; we will stick together, helping one another. Tomorrow will be great as long as we stand together in love. Therefore, tonight is the night you make a new resolve to put up your best fight. Tonight is the night you pull out those ideas you have hidden away, coated in dust; tonight is the night you reaffirm your belief in yourself because it is not over with you. I believe in you, I have faith in you, I have confidence in you because I was once like you – hopeless, frustrated, confused – but in the midst of my tragic circumstance I found myself, I found hope and I rekindled my dreams. Fan that dwindling flame of your dreams to life, jump-start that career, kick-start that ambition. The sky is not your limit and no one can stop you because this is your moment, and in your moment, anything is possible.

RELAX ... B-R-E-A-T-H-E ... LIFE IS GOOD

$\mathcal{I}$ was reading a book the other day by a very famous author, and she wrote that she was afraid of becoming poor in her old age. She's not alone, as research has shown that a lot of people, both rich and poor, have this fear. That makes me wonder: how much money do we really need to quench our fear of poverty, how much money do we need to give us peace of mind? How much luxury would satiate our soul and quench our desire for more?

A friend once told me that people are motivated by two factors: fear and greed. Either we are afraid of being poor and are driven to acquire more wealth, or we are motivated by greed and have the desire to acquire more wealth than we really need. Either way, we are forced to do something that ordinarily we wouldn't want to do, something outside our true nature. Greed and fear are not natural human states, they originate from errors in judgement, and our true nature is based on truth, not error. Thoughts are generated within the human mind. The mind can be influenced by positive or negative thoughts. Negative thoughts are judgemental errors, and can be corrected by truth, since truth is positive thought. As truth resides within the mind, truth is inherent. Therefore, the solution to the fear of poverty lies within us. If we look within, if we search the deep recesses of our minds, if we contemplate and meditate, we will find that the good life, the life that is free from anxiety, fear, greed, and insecurity, is and has always been within our grasp. We were designed to reign over our world, and just as the scriptures remind us that "the kingdom of God is within us,"[1] so the things we search for without have always been within us. The answers to our fears, worries, and anxieties lie within our grasp. We are the answers to all our problems.

We live in an abundant universe that is ever sharing its resources. Think about water, sand, the leaves on the trees, the air that we breathe, the sky up above; everything nature supplies is in profusion, it's always in abundant supply. There is no lack or limitations! So, if we have everything in abundant supply, why are we anxious? At what point did we realise that the future cannot be trusted? How did we come to dwell on the uncertainties of tomorrow?

When we happened on the scene, initially, there was order, love, and cordial relationships, but suddenly we woke up to an anxious reality, a perception that these resources may not be enough for everyone, and so the scrambling began. We have forgotten that we did not put ourselves on this planet; neither did we bring these resources with us. We met them here, and that is where we will leave them when we die; no matter how much we try to gather, we can't take anything with us when we leave. So, isn't this like the proverbial fetching water with a sieve? If the more we gather, the more we lose at the end of our lives, what is the point of worrying about not gathering enough when what we need is just basic necessities?

I am not advocating a hermetic life, that choice is up to you. I am only reminding you that life could be more fun if we focus on savouring the pleasant moments life has to offer and fearlessly express our divine purposes. Many of us breeze through life without actually living. All our experiences are struggles, fights, and worries. We forget that we are here to experience and enjoy life.

There is a tourism promotional video that depicts the wonderful scenery of the beautiful province of Alberta, in Canada. In the video, we see pictures of rivers, mountains, wild life, and happy people engulfed in one breath, savouring the moment. At the end of the video, the awestricken viewer is reminded to "remember to breathe."

Many times, we are so engrossed in life's activities, challenges, duties, and obligations, we forget the very simple act of living our lives ... we forget to breathe. We came here to experience and enjoy life, to feel and express love, to share joy, peace, harmony, and beauty, and to be the very best of ourselves ... but we forget the purpose of life – which is simply to live.

Our original agenda is to express the very best of ourselves and to have fun while living life. But we tend to forget this plan because we are overridden by ambition, greed, and the fear of not-enough-ness. Life is not as hard as we think. The scriptures remind us that we should "be anxious for nothing,"[2] for our future is guaranteed to be safe and secure. Fear is the root cause of all evil. Your future was guaranteed when you showed up on the scene; you are not constrained to live in lack and limitation. You were defined as a self-sustaining entity, capable of creating and re-creating your present and your future, from your health to your wealth. You were made to lack nothing! Occasionally, I have accidentally cut myself with a knife or a razor blade and have forgotten to apply medication, but that didn't stop the wound from healing on its own. This shows that our bodies are self-sustaining. Man is made wholly complete; everything we need to succeed in life came with us when we were born.

A person might be born under heavily disadvantaged financial circumstances, and their poverty might run into 3rd and 4th generations. Yet, in some cases, one among them whose determination sets him apart from the rest, changes the course of the family history. He tells himself that nothing is impossible and he rises up from the ashes, from the doldrums, from the history of lack and limitations set up by his ancestors, and becomes a phenomenon, an enigma, an icon of success for future generations. This tells us that you are not defined by your background, colour, race, or family history. You are defined by your thought. You can be a success in any career, in any circumstance or situation. So, don't fight, struggle, or compete with one another. There is enough for everyone. Above all, you have a specific task, and you have been equipped with skills that will make you excel in this task. So, stay focused, be in harmony with one another, and worry less about the future, because it is already guaranteed to be safe. Be yourself at all times, play the role you were called to play. Life is fun, we all are here to have fun – to live in the now, and remember to … B-r-e-a-t-h-e.

In order to thrive and be free of fear of privation in the future, we ought to emulate nature. Everything nature provides is meant to circulate. The freshness of water comes when it flows downstream; the air we breathe becomes fresh when it circulates. The tree lets its leaves fall to the ground; this nourishes the ground, providing nutrients for the tree. Nature is self-sustaining; it is ever giving and never holding back. This same principle applies to wealth. The more you give, the more you get, a life of sharing is a life of having. In his book "*A Meaning to Life,*" Michael Ruse wrote, "The only truly happy person is the person giving to others."

I know some people will say "hah ha-ha, there you go, sounding like one of those prosperity preachers." But, I was born smack in the middle of eight children. My dad was an Anglican priest whose paycheck was nothing to write home about. In our little home we shared food, clothing, everything. We barely had enough, but we never lacked anything. In my adult life, I had a good career in advertising, and through those exciting and successful years, I never stopped sharing and many times got in trouble for sharing too much, but still, I never lacked and I was never worried about where the next dollar would come from. After many years of practicing giving, I realize that *"flow"* is the magic word that ensures a continuous stream of income. There is no amount of money you put away in your savings that will be enough to meet all your future needs, you will still be poor someday if that lump sum is not multiplied in one way or another; you don't get rich by saving, no one does. That is why people give it away. You give money away in investments, you keep it flowing when you make purchases, when you give to charity, when you spend it on yourself – flow is the word, keep money moving around, keep it flowing. Don't lock it up in some secret savings. You can't tie it down, because it has a life of its own and often it takes up wings and flies, that is what we found in the book of proverbs.[3]

Everyone has a right to wealth; you were designed to be successful, rich, and to be in perfect health. Your perception of having limitations is wrong; you have been put here on Earth to experience and enjoy life! Your life has been guaranteed by a higher power that understands you more than you can ever understand yourself. So, why are you blinded by anxiousness? Why have you allowed fear to paralyze your judgement? Why are you worried? What do you see when you receive your paycheck with very little left after all the taxes and deductions? What do you see when you are hit by a sudden financial crisis? What do you see when you get laid off your job? Your perception determines your expectation and your expectations can never rise above the limitations you set above them. We are the creators of our own destinies; we shape our future through our thoughts and limited perceptions.

People scrimp and save in fear of uncertainty. The secret of a secured financial future lies in the *"flow"* – be a channel, a transit point, a conduit for money, it's in the giving that you get. This is the secret, the security, the guarantee of a secured future. Charles Haanel, in his book, *The Master Key System*, said, "We cannot obtain what we lack if we tenaciously cling to what we have." We live in a universe that is governed by laws, the law of circularity is empirically evident, what we give, we receive.

The things we fear create strong holds over our lives. It is true that when you don't have money saved up for your old age, you might end up in the streets, but what guarantees that those monies put away will remain safe until you need them? What is the guarantee that your bank will remain in business? What guarantees that you'll always have perfect health? For in just one quick swoop, an illness can wipe out your entire savings, your bank may run into bankruptcy, your job may be gone. There are a thousand and one factors that can take out your savings; in fact, it is the thought of these factors that is the probable cause of your anxiety. You can only enjoy the future if you are in good health at the present and you can only be in good health at the present if you are not anxious about the future. Some of our fears are baseless. I'll tell you a story.

As a child growing up, I was very superstitious. I don't know how this came about because I had a strong religious upbringing that disregarded superstition. Anyway, I had this belief that bats were witches and that it was ominous to have bats around your house. At this time, I was living in a rented apartment with my younger sister, and every night at about 2 am, we would hear noises that sounded like bats on our roof. When we heard these noises, we would jump out of our beds and pray, we'd cast out the demon bats. We did all manner of spiritual gymnastics, yet this continued for about six months until one night, after praying so hard for about an hour, we were sweating profusely, so I opened the windows for some fresh air, but just then I noticed that the noise was right above my head, so I looked up. Adjacent to our window was the object of our terror – my neighbour's rusty, old ceiling fan. For the past six months, we'd been having a power shortage that resulted in power sharing that started at 2 am every morning. When the electricity kicked in at 2 am, the rusty old fan would start whirling, the whirling sounded like bat noises. The poor old fan needed some grease, but little did it know that it had been scaring the hell out of its neighbours. The moral of this story is, the things we fear are not always what they seem when we walk up to them. If we face situations fearlessly, more often than not, there are no situations to face. There is an ancient saying that "courage contains both genius and magic." The power to neutralize our fears lies in our courage to walk up to them and face them squarely. Fear not the future, for it holds the very best for you. In the Holy Scriptures we read: "the thought I think towards you saith the lord are thoughts of good not evil, to give you a hope and a future."[4] The infinite spirit has your back and has made provision for all your supplies.

We have a dynamic life force within us, a force that is unstoppable and uninhibited. Our future is not tied to any circumstance, situation, or person. We hail from the divine, our potential is limitless. Our thoughts are malleable, how we want our future to be is within our control because our thoughts determine our actions and our actions result in our circum-stances and situations. The choice you make this very moment will determine whether your tomorrow will be spent in abject poverty or profuse abundance. Hoarding and saving will not guarantee you a better future, neither will worrying do you any good. Rather, join the flow of the universe, let go your fears of poverty and insecurity. Be fearless in handling your finances; trust the infinite, for he is the source of all your needs. Christ said, "which of you by taking thought can add one cubit unto his stature?"[5] No one! We worry about not having enough for the future when today is yet to be lived. An anxious mindset takes away joy, it affects our attitude toward life. We become aggressive, grumpy, ruthless, and selfish, and often, yes, very often, these vices could lead to living a miserable life. Some people have gone to jail because of silly mistakes they made when driven by fear of not having enough. We are here to enjoy life, and to express the very presence of the infinite as we travel through this journey called life. You are fully equipped to live the best life you deserve. So, give, share, love, be happy, be confident that you have more than enough. There is a Sanskrit saying that "we only keep what we give away." Partake of the giving-ness of the universe, partake of the sharing, partake of the flow. You are limitless in your potential, so be fearless, be courageous, be strong, the future is already yours. At this moment, you are the best, no one can do the things you were meant to do, so do not be anxious about tomorrow because your life is already guaranteed by the one who made you. But if you feel the pressure of life mounting and you are beginning to lose your foothold, just take a moment and ... B-r-e-a-t-h-e.

ARISTOTLE, RENE DESCARTES AND KC O'KERRY ON THE REAL MEANING OF LIFE

*T*wo years ago, my uncle passed away. The agony of his demise triggered an old thought that I had suppressed for a very long time. You see, when I was eight, my immediate elder brother died. His death stirred a conundrum which my perplexed little soul galvanized. Some of the questions aroused in my consciousness at that time were: what is the real meaning of life? Why are we here on Earth? What is our purpose of existence? Is there more to human existence than to dream, achieve those dreams, and die? What is this "I" that I call myself?

You will agree with me that these questions are pretty complex, especially for a 10 year-old; yet, I have grappled with them since my childhood. In search of answers, I read tons of books, studied philosophers and philosophies, joined several religious and spiritual groups, all to no avail; the answers remain elusive. In my quest for answers, I found similar minds who have tried to unravel these mysteries.

Rene Descartes, the renowned French philosopher, declared "cogito ergo sum," meaning "I think therefore I am," that is, "I exist!" a statement that confirms consciousness. But something vital is missing from Descartes' declaration. Who is this "I" he referred to? Some may say Descartes, in calling his existence into doubt, was not referring to an inner being, but rather to his physical consciousness. But assuming we accept the fact that we exist as physical beings, this "I" needs further explanation! Or could it be that he was referring to something within himself. Obviously, our duality is evident in our thoughts, for we hold arguments within ourselves; but if man does not have a dual personality, who is having those conversations within man, why does it seem that there is another being that holds a contrary opinion to our intentions?

Descartes came to a conclusion about the reality of his existence, and thus declared that no matter how much he denied his reality, there was one thing he knew for sure – he was conscious of his existence. Without any reasonable doubt, I agree with Descartes, but beyond that, I would want to know who or what this entity we call "I" really is. Who am I? Why do I feel like I am encased within another being? What is the reason for and the purpose of my existence? Where will I go when I exit this realm?

Now, if we can't define who or what man really is, and we cannot identify what we often refer to as the "I," maybe we should examine why we are here, perhaps it will lead us to our personal identity. Most religions point to a place of eternal bliss, thus explaining Earth to be transitional. But why transition through Earth in the first place? What is the purpose or benefit of this transition? Some say we are here to learn human virtues such as goodness, love, beauty, and justice, so that we can control our bodies and our behaviour. But this is useless because our physical body does not come with us when we die! It is therefore pertinent to ask how these experiences can be transferred to the next realm if our physical bodies do not survive death. Is it possible that another being that is conscious of these experiences does exist, and that it is this non-physical being that holds the records and thus transfers these experiences or virtues to the next realm? This argument is begging the question! So, let's step back and take another look. If we agree that there must be something else that records and transfers human experience to the next plane of existence, then we can conclusively say that there must be something else that does exist beside this physical body!

But wait a minute, before we draw an early conclusion on this discussion, let's talk some more about the meaning and purpose of life because it may give us some insight as to who the entity "I" really is.

Aristotle suggested that "happiness" is the ultimate goal every person seeks when he or she engages in any activity. He said that all the actions we take tend to lead us directly or indirectly to happiness. Aristotle's theory resonates with current trends, as people seem to be more concerned with pleasurable experiences than the deep contemplations that he also considered to be the highest form of human experience. People want luxuries, comfortable cars and homes, so, maybe Aristotle has a point. However, because humans favour pleasurable experiences over a contemplative life does not make pleasurable living our ultimate reason for existence. For if happiness is the purpose of all human existence, then life must be worthless because happiness is relative; for example, the happiness of a sociopath is the pain of the victim.

I perceive man to be too intelligible to be satisfied with mere pursuit of pleasurable experiences, because we have a mind that is introspective and contemplative, we aim for higher ideals than we sometimes achieve, and we yearn for understanding, perfection, beauty, love, and justice. Therefore there must be more to human life than merely happiness. And just as water finds its course, so it is with the urge to search for meaning, purpose, and expression. There is a tugging in everybody's heart, constantly urging us to seek, to search, and to inquire.

For, if we had no consciousness of another realm, a perfect world that exists outside the present realm, a place where there are no boundaries, inhibitions, or limitations, a world where peace, love, and joy reign supreme, we wouldn't be yearning for it. Man is spiritual, and as such attracts spiritual experiences; we are constantly yearning for our spiritual origin. We are constantly expressing our spirituality in our thoughts and actions. For instance, when faced with an insurmountable challenge, we turn inward to seek guidance; when we have a health issue that defies a medical solution, we turn to prayer, when we have an emotional disturbance that is pulling us apart, we are pressed to meditate. All these inclinations indicate that there is something bigger, stronger, and more powerful within us! This explains that there exists another life form that is omnipresent, omnipotent, and omniscient dwelling within us. In other words, man is a synchronicity of two life forms, one visible, the other invisible.

Let us return to our first argument. We don't know who or what this "I" really is. Neither do we know the purpose of our existence, since I have argued that happiness alone is too vague a concept to define our reason for existence. However, we are conscious of another presence dwelling within us. A clue can be derived from the greatest teacher in human history; in the Gospel of John 6:38, Jesus said: "For I came down from heaven, not to do mine own will, but the will of him that sent me." This means that, for every man, there is a reason or purpose of existence. Jesus' purpose was to teach a new message; your purpose or mine would be different from Jesus' purpose. But, there is a reason that you and I are here on this planet, especially at this time; there is a plan, there is a grand design. The goal of some people might be to create a fantastic product that would transform all humanity, other people might dream of a revolution that would change mankind. For every man, there is a purpose, an ideal, a goal. No matter what condition you are in, no matter

what situation that is holding you back, no matter what circumstance is getting you entangled and frustrated, know that you
have been uniquely created to fulfil a purpose. The purpose of
human existence is not just to experience and exit life, no. We
are not tourists from some distant galaxy, we are creators, we
are here to input and impact, we are here to make a difference,
to help develop human consciousness, to create and to become
more aware of our divine potentials; we are here to shine the
light of truth and to express divinity within us. It doesn't matter
in what job or profession you find yourself, it doesn't matter
that you don't have royal blood running in your veins, or that
you don't have great academic qualifications. For as long as you
will exist in this scene called life, there is a task, there is a
purpose, there is a job for you. You are not ordinary; you are a
unique manifestation of the infinite. You are here to serve a
purpose, you are here to meet a need, and you are part of a
divine plan and purpose. Whatever you decide to do, as long as
it brings you happiness and fulfillment, as long as it meets a
need, as long as it's good with God and good with man, that is
your divine purpose. In this same line of thinking, Paul wrote in
the Philippians 4:8, "Finally, brethren, whatsoever things are
true, whatsoever things are honest, whatsoever things are just,
whatsoever things are pure, whatsoever things are lovely, whatsoever things are of good report; if there be any virtue, and if
there be any praise, think on these things. Contemplate on these
things, focus on these pursuits, for they are aligned with the
divine design." Your life is not an accident; you were created
specifically for a purpose. What is that thing that is pressing
strongly in your heart, what is that idea that is burning hot
within you, that is seeking expression, what is that creative urge
that is keeping you awake all night? That is divinity calling,
don't hold back, don't turn it off or turn it down, don't give it
up. You've got to let it out. All your talents, gifts, and capacities
are meant for expression. You are made unique for the purpose

of expressing yourself in that special way only you can. So, what are you waiting for? "Just do it!" as Nike would say.

For now, let's forget about where we will be headed when our task here on earth is done. Let's focus on what's got to be done here. Your only task, your only purpose, the only reason you showed up on the scene is to be the best that you can be, so go for it and shine ... be who you were designated to be.

A MESSAGE FOR NEW IMMIGRANTS:
IT'S ALRIGHT AND IT'S ALL GOOD

I see you sitting over there, a graduate, from one of the best universities in your country. Life was good and comfortable until a recent downturn in your finances. It seems like some weird bad dream, yet this is your new reality. Now listen, what you see now is temporary; it will change for the better. I've been there and I know that you can get back on your feet again, just as I did. Trust me when I say that, even in the midst of these challenges ... it's all right and it's all good!

I can see you want to give up, but why do you want to give up? It's not over until you say so. You can turn your tragedy to triumph. Your limitation is determined by your expectation. You cannot have what you never expected. Clement W. Stone said, "What the mind of man can conceive and believe, the mind of man can achieve through positive mental attitude" You can be what you will yourself to be. You are destined for the skies, you are a winner! It's not where you are right now but where you want to be that counts, and right now you are in transition to your destiny. So cheer up and smile, and say with confidence, "It's alright and it's all good. Oh come on, say it like you really mean it ... "It's alright and it's all good!"

The best of us is revealed in our weakest moments, challenges bring out our inner strength, latent skills are exposed, abilities we never knew existed are revealed. In the words of Friedrich Nietzsche he said "What does not destroy me makes me stronger." Consider this as your gestation period, the period that will birth the new you, the transformed you, the renewed you, the you, you've always wanted to be. I am not offering you vain words of encouragement, I am telling you tried and tested facts. I had it rough, too, in my beginning, and I was down there just as you are for several months. I was without work, my funds were running low, there were no family or friends I could call on, it seemed like I had come to the end of the road. There were days I'd lie on my bed late at night and cry. But even though I was depressed I was not defeated, I was cast down but not conquered, under pressure but not overwhelmed. From the rubble of my broken dreams my fingers struck out the sign of victory with doggedness that seemed to say No! I will not back down! No! I will not give up. Because I knew that in due time I would be saying … It's alright and it's all good!

In retrospect, I am happy that I had some hard times. If it were not for the hard times I would never know I had the latent skills of a writer, if not for the hard times I would never know I was good at math, if not for the hard times I would never know I was an outstanding songwriter. Desperation brings out the best in us. So rise up my friend, there are skills within you that are dying to be revealed. This experience is meant for your good, your growth, your development, and your expansion. Your tomorrow can only be greater than your yesterday if you choose to make today different. You are stronger than you know and smarter than you think. Don't let doubt and fear becloud your thinking, reassure yourself time and time again by saying … It's alright and it's all good!

Henry Wadsworth Longfellow said "Perseverance is a great

element of success, if you knock long enough and loud enough you surely must wake up somebody." Success comes to those who wait, and patience is a virtue. But resilience is even more important because what you see now is fleeting, this challenge will soon be over and just as the Bible says, "weeping may endure for a night but joy comes in the morning"[1]. My friend, your bigger, better, and brighter side is on its way and soon you will be saying ... It's alright and it's all good!

My dad once had a bunch of free range ducks. Once in a while he would trim their wings to keep them on the ground so they didn't fly all over the place. One day a hawk came by, swooped on a duckling and tried to get away with it. There was a brief fight between the mother duck and the hawk, but the hawk got away with the duckling. Unbeknown to my dad, the mother duck had missed the last wing trimming session. So she spread out her fully grown wings and flew after the hawk. She's disappeared for about half an hour, but finally reappeared with her baby clutched tightly in her jaws. This story shows that you can always get back what is yours by right.

Success is not an exclusive right of just a few people; it's for everyone who seeks it, for everyone who strives, for everyone who earnestly desires it. Your hunger for change has created your current life experience, therefore, now is the time you've been waiting for, now is the time to stand on your feet, now is the time to fight the fight of faith. Those who seek will find, for those who knock the door will open, when you ask it shall be given, there are no limitations in the resources of the infinite. When you persevere, it won't be long before the whole world shouts with you saying... It's alright and it's all good.

Whatever you are going through right now is just a temporary distraction, so don't let it get to you! Focus on your dreams, focus on your goals, and focus on your aspirations. Circumstances don't define who you are; it's who you are that defines your circumstances! As Ritu Ghatourey said, "The world will tell you who you are, until you tell the world who you really are." Your future is in your hands; you can be what you want to be. No matter what difficulties you find in your current life experience, sit back and relax because very soon you will be saying… It's alright and it's all good.

THE POWER OF BEAUTY CONSCIOUSNESS: WOMAN, YOU ARE BEAUTIFUL

*S*he's 5 foot 2, she is as beautiful as she can be, a woman that causes men to stop and stare, a beauty so amazing it renders men speechless, a woman every man would want to have for a wife, a natural beauty, full bodied ... but she thinks she's fat. She's become a statistic of the self-hating women labeled "plus size." Her confidence has long been eroded, now she lives in fear of a nonexistent fact promoted by ambitious salesmen and product manufacturers. Every time she looks in the mirror, she's overwhelmed; it's like a knife cutting deep into an open wound. When she sees fashion models on TV and in magazines, she's constantly reminded of her weight and size; but in reality, is she really fat? In real life, fashion models don't come close to what we see on television and in those glossy magazines. Often, pictures are edited; hip bones, collar bones, and ribs are all cleverly refined with Photoshop to make the women look more elegant!

In Linda Lewis Alexander's book, *New Dimensions in Women's Health* (2007), females account for 90% of the estimated eight million sufferers of eating disorders. Every 62 minutes at least one person dies as a direct result of an eating disorder. This is because many women want to attain that perfect body! A perfection that is not realistic! There is no such thing as a perfect body – tall, short, fat or thin, black, white or yellow – you are beautiful just the way you are! Beauty comes from within, it is a consciousness. The world will tell you who you are but it's only you who can define who you really are.

Now is the time to live and be who you really want to be. Your beauty lies in your knowing, appreciating, acknowledging, and celebrating your true self; you are beautiful just the way you are. In this moment, you have this great body as a gift. You've got to appreciate what you have! Your beauty consciousness has nothing to do with money, it has nothing to do with your career or position or your ability to wearing popular brands, it's in the realization of who you really are in the now! Your glory is in your knowing you are perfection made real. Even the Bible said "you are fearfully and wonderfully made."[1] Your beauty is immeasurable and indescribable. Sisters, you've got everything going for you: your looks, the way you walk, the way you talk. You are graceful when you saunter down the street in the evening sun, the guys can't help but slow down their cars, take off their sun shades, just to catch a glimpse of your curves and your backside drumming rhythmically to your footsteps, oh, I tell you … woman … you are beautiful.

In order to enjoy life, you need to be happy. Now, happiness comes when you acknowledge and celebrate your true self. Forget about what people feel, think, or say about you. Live in the now! Savour every single moment. Never compare yourself with others. Remember that we are not all the same; the world would be absolutely boring if everyone was tall or short, big or small, fat or thin, black or white, we each have a uniqueness, and we each add color to the spectrum of the human race! A fundamental question you must consider at all times is "are you happy with who you are?" This question must not be based on a comparison with others, or with unattained goals, rather, it should be a deep-seated feeling. Do you feel good about yourself? If the answer is "yes," then you recognize the perfect lady that you are! Self-appreciation boosts confidence, which in turn creates a vibration that reflects as beauty. Every woman has something special, something that is unique to each individual. Look at yourself in the mirror, is that really you? You probably haven't noticed those natural long eyelashes, do you see them? How about that cute smile on your face? These long years of self-criticism and a focus on body weight, skin color, and all that you don't have, have taken a toll on you! Take a good look at yourself in a mirror; can't you see how beautiful you are? Please believe me when I say … woman … you are beautiful!

Female models have been getting thinner and thinner over the past 100 years. A century ago, the ideal body shape of a woman was fleshy and full-figured. As the models get thinner, more women and younger girls are getting frustrated and feeling unhappy about their own natural body shapes. In one statistic, the average model is taller and weighs 23%, or almost a quarter, less than the average woman who is 5' 4" and weighs 148 lbs. Most retail stores in America carry size 14 dresses and smaller, while the average American woman wears size 14 and larger. The human race is evolving, body sizes have increased, yet the media has made people believe that being thin is the ideal, and thinness has been associated with success, wealth, and health.

Consider the women society has celebrated and adored; they are not self-absorbed in skin color or their body weight or the texture of their hair; rather, they glowed in their various careers, the world couldn't help but celebrate them. Starting with Florence Nightingale and moving to Michelle Obama, from Mother Theresa to Oprah Winfrey, these women suggest personality and strength, what they evoke is beyond outer beauty! The world is looking for that kind of beauty, a beauty that changes the world positively, a beauty that touches hearts and affects lives. You've got to wake up, Sisters; you've got to turn your back on these trends. You've got to be you in order to get to where you want to be! You've got the looks, you've got the style, you've got everything that makes you that perfect woman, so when you hear the media and their supporters clamoring for their wrong ideals, you've got to take your stand and yell at the top of your voice! "Woman ... you are beautiful!"

Life is a game of giving and receiving. The thought you give attention to, comes into your life experience. If the whole world is celebrating mediocrity, would you want to buy that? Of course not! So, when you wake up every morning, you've got to tell yourself how beautiful you are, because no one else will! In fact, the world will tear you down, ridicule you, and pull you apart. So, trust your inner counsel when it gives you this reassurance. Let the whole world go to blazes. You have one task, which is to live your life to the best of your ability. Let no one stand in your way; you are your own standard. What you don't realize at this moment is that you are prettier than you feel, and smarter than you know. What you are going through right now is just a clarifying moment, by the time this experience is over you will be well-defined, better, brighter, and stronger. This new you will open doors not only to your true beautiful self but to other opportunities that hitherto were considered unattainable. This is why beauty is associated with success. A higher positive self-consciousness leads to confidence, and confidence translates to success. Young women who find their confidence gain the strength to perform exploits. Don't let anyone run your life for you, take the front seat! Take charge and tell everyone who cares to listen, that ... woman ... you are beautiful!

There is a place for every woman, irrespective of the size of her birthday suit. We are all connected with divinity. It is the plan of the infinite for everyone to be happy. The type of birthday suit you came in doesn't matter. What you did and what you achieve during your life is what counts. You've got to put a smile on your face every day, be happy, look good within the assets that you have, and look forward to every day as an opportunity to celebrate you. Celebrate every moment because life is good. What happened to you yesterday doesn't matter; what is happening to you now is the most important part of your life. Life is in the now, so live in the now! Right now you are happy, right now you know you are beautiful, right now you know you have potentials no one else has and that no one can do things exactly the same way that you would. You are unique. You are the best that ever was, ever is, and ever shall be; you are special. You are not ashamed of your looks, you are proud of your skin color, you are proud to be a full-bodied woman and, yes, you are proud of your curves! There's nothing more to add to your cup of awesomeness, so cheer up, Lady, and say with me … woman … you are beautiful!

I want you to realize that beauty is just a consciousness. Your peers, family members, colleagues, and the media may create situations that do not resonate with the new you, but you've got to wake up to your true self; no one else can do this for you. The world is yet to see and experience the real you, the true you, the beautiful you. There's no one like you and there is never going to be anyone like you. You've got to focus on your attributes, focus on your plans and purposes, and all the other things you've always wanted to do or to be. Life is yours for the taking and the winner takes all. Let go of every negative thought, of thoughts that demean you, of thoughts that remind you of who you are not; of course, that makes sense because you cannot be who you are not! Because you are not what you are not! Ha … ha. Build your self-confidence day after day by holding positive thoughts. Affirm your beauty. Affirm your strength. Affirm every positive aspect of your being! You are what you think you are. Whatever thought you hold in your consciousness manifests in your life experience. See yourself as the queen that you are, and you will be treated as a queen; don't let anyone talk you down. You are the best that is and ever shall be, you are gorgeous, you are beautiful, oh yes you are. Know this, believe this, understand this, live this, and above all, never, ever, forget that … woman … you are beautiful!

LET YOUR PASSION LEAD YOU TO SUCCESS

I guess this must have happened to you, too, because it has happened to almost everyone in the early stages of their careers. You run into an old schoolmate; he looks exquisite, from his finely cut hair to his polished leather shoes, that contrast with your ungroomed beard and rumpled blazer. Obviously, your classmate is not "just doing well," he is flourishing. Suddenly, you feel a pang of jealousy in the pit of your stomach; you just want to run away, fast, very fast. And the questions that kept running through your head as you steal away are: "Where did I go wrong?" "How come I am not as successful as my classmate?" "How come I always seem to come short of success at every twist and turn in life?" "Am I doomed to be the dredge of society?" Obviously, you are jealous of your friend's success; you wish you had what he has! But wait a minute. Was it that you are incapable of achieving success, or does fate smile at everybody else but you? Now listen: as for the misfortune part, only very few people can lay a claim to that, because many people count misfortune as their catalyst for growth, so that leaves you without any excuses.

So, where exactly did you go wrong? Does it have to do with

your low aspirations and poor goal-setting? Probably, because when we look at life principles, we see that we get only what we give. In order to attain a goal, we must exert some effort. These efforts are the "givings," and the consequence of giving is our state of affairs. So, if all things are equal, you probably did not set high enough goals, in other words, where you are now is where you've always wanted to be, because life gave you the exact measure you asked for.

I remember when I was a young adult, my uncle, told me to aim high, high enough that even if I fail, I'll still be succeeding. He said, "aim at the stars, you will fall on the clouds, aim at the clouds you will fall on the tree tops, but if you aim at the tree tops you may end up on the ground." He said, "give yourself a chance to succeed at life, and that chance starts with your mind."

Your thoughts, your goals, your dreams, your intentions, all start from the mind. Where you are today was the height you contemplated some time ago, nothing more, nothing less. There is no such thing as a stroke of luck or some lucky angel smiling down on you. Whatever you hold in your consciousness is what manifests in your life experience. Let me tell you a story.

There was this kid from a very poor family. His parents could not buy him the toy guitar he clamoured for on his 3rd birthday. So, one day he found some strings and some scraps of wood, and with the help of his dad, he made a guitar. Day after day we see him bent over his guitar, practicing and envisioning a future in the entertainment business. Soon, with a little savings put together, he buys his first real guitar and presses on even harder, practicing. A few years later, we see him headlining the news; he is the new whiz kid on the block, they call him the master for he is the master of his craft. Large stadiums cannot contain his performances; the bright lights and his allure garner people from far and wide. He has become a true success. His poor beginning is completely obliterated. His lack of funding could not stop him, his lack of formal education could not stop him, the absence of a godfather could not stop him. He is dynamic, he tore through his circumstances like they were nonexistent; he fought against odds and triumphed, all because he had a picture of his ideal in mind. He was focused.

No one, I repeat, no one, is incapable of success. Our failure is mostly due to distractions. Everyone has an idea, a passion, something that consumes his or her thoughts when he or she is alone. But often we get distracted by the success of others. Suddenly we want to emulate their business ideas, we want to copy what they are doing, and we want to be like them, and so we dump our original ideas and jump onto their bandwagons, forgetting that everyone has been given a niche, a special gift, a talent. Now, I am not saying it's not good to aspire to what others have done, in fact, emulation is one of the methods of self-development, but I am saying that you must remain faithful to your ideal. Don't dump your idea just because your neighbour's idea seems more appealing. Stick to your dream, hang in there, strive to perfect it and it will blossom. Focus on your passion, expand that vision of yours and believe in yourself.

Of course, there will always be people who are smarter or more creative or more skillful than you are. But you are unique in your own special way, and your uniqueness makes you exceptional. No one is going to do things the way you do or say things in the particular way that you would. You are different, and that difference is what makes you special. For instance, there are a million and one comedians out there, but each one does different things or says things differently. I love Eddie Murphy movies because he is funny; he says funny things and acts really funny. But I also love Adam Sandler because he is also very funny and he says things in a funny way. These two people are at the top of their game and both are extremely successful. But what if Adam Sandler had said "comedy is an African American thing and Eddie Murphy seems to be the one everybody wants to see, so I am quitting." Do you think we would have enjoyed the laughter Adam Sandler has brought into our homes? Of course not!

Stop belittling yourself. I can't seem to say this enough: there is room at the top for everyone. You are a winner! You are great, you are awesome, and you are talented. Strive on, push on, the winning line is just around the corner. Find your passion and stick to it!

Two reasons guarantee your success in a venture that is rooted in your passion: (1) You will be doing what you really love to do and that leads to total commitment, and commitment is an essential ingredient of success. (2) Because you are passionate about what you love, it leads to focused attention, and a focused attention inevitably leads to success. When people pay attention to the things they love to do, they turn out very high quality product. People want beautiful and perfect stuff, and that can come only from people with passion for their works.

There is no effort, be it good or bad, which will not yield a result, if you put a focused attention on it. It is a law. So practice; put in lots of effort, it's the key to perfection. Spend time on the things you really love to do and you'll be good at them. Ask a man who plays the piano by ear, he'll tell you it's all about practice. The master practitioner today was once an apprentice; it's the amount of practice and dedication that puts him in the master's shoes. If you practice for at least one hour every day, you'll be amazed at how much you'll accomplish in a year. So, the question is, do you really want that thing that you say you desire? Do you want that change? Are you willing to lay everything aside and sacrifice time at the altar of your passion? Your mindset will determine how far you go. If you think you can, then of course you can. I need you to pay attention to this, because when I got this epiphany, I stopped chasing after financial gains, and concentrated on doing what gave me the greatest joy and satisfaction. The secret of success does not lie in dabbling into every business venture; rather, it's in doing what you really love to do.

When you observe people and their hobbies, you will notice that while they engage in a job or a career, they often set aside time and money to invest in their hobbies. After a while, these hobbies become full blown businesses due to the level of attention they have received. You will also find these people to be happier and more relaxed when they are engaged in their hobbies compared to when they are engaged in their regular jobs. Now some people may say, "I don't know what my passions are," or "I don't know how to turn my passion into a business." Though this might be rare, here is how to determine or define your passion. The first thing you must do is ask yourself these basic questions:

1. What do I really, really love doing that gets me excited every time, and I never get tired of doing it?
2. Can this passion be turned into a business?
3. How ambitious is this plan?

You might never have thought about your passion in this context. So, determine how big or how successful you want to be. Visualize your future and immerse yourself deeply in the experience. If you don't like your perceptual ideas, then this is the perfect time to expand your vision. After you have answered these questions, work like crazy to get to that height you have determined. Two things you must always keep in mind are *hard work* and a *focused mind*. These two ingredients go hand in hand in order to achieve success. This brings to mind a verse written by Henry Wadsworth Longfellow[1]: "The heights by great men reached and kept were not attained by sudden flight, but they, while their companions slept, were toiling upward in the night."

There are no short cuts to success. You must roll up your sleeves and dig in. And not just dig, but dig like crazy.

My high school teacher often said "the butcher never minds the flies." In other words, a focused mind never acknowledges distractions. If you set your goals big enough and high enough in the career of your passion, you'll be amazed at (a) how fast you get to where you want to be and (b) how successful you will become. Never bother about what other people are doing or saying. You are the most important person on the face of the earth. Only you have been given this mandate to do the things you are passionate about. No one can do it better than you can; you were chosen specifically for this task and you are perfect for the job. Stay in the moment and hold on to your passion, it's only a matter of time before your efforts will yield success. If you are fully engaged in your passion, the thoughts of your friends doing better than you will never cross your mind, even if they are vacationing on Mars or have a reserved suite in the White House. You have a gift; the world is waiting for you to unfold it into magnificence.

There are no limitations to what you can be, do, or have. You can have anything as long as you have a strong desire for it. That dream, that idea you have been tinkering with for years, is possible, don't be afraid to carry it out, it is possible to achieve it. You may not have the brain power of Albert Einstein, or the creative mastery of Michelangelo, but you have something that is unique that none of the above-mentioned persons did have.

Take the case of an 81 year old South African grandmother, Esther Mahlangu, who stands tall among artistic greats, despite the fact that she had no formal education, had no financial support from anyone, and was not exceptionally gifted at birth. By pulling inspiration from her environment, her culture, her life experiences, she created masterpieces that British Airways, BMW, and her community in South Africa could not resist. You too, my friend, are somebody special; you have something within you waiting to unravel, you are unique, you are one in a million, and you are outstandingly awesome. The world is waiting to see, to hear, and to experience your creative genius. Now is your moment, now is your opportunity, and now is the time you have been waiting for. Don't let this moment slip by, because the world is counting on you to be the you you've always wanted to be. So, wake up to the reality of being you and let your passion take over.

THE CHARGE

$\mathcal{D}$reams, they say, are the wings of the mind, we can fly any time. We have been endowed with abilities to be the best that we can be. Therefore, nothing is impossible when we set our mind to any endeavor.

The limitations we experience in life are only a reflection of our negative perceptions; when we change our negative perceptions, our good will be manifest. What I mean by this is that we are more than who or what we think we are.

Our suffering, and the delays in achieving our dreams, goals, aspirations, are due to a misunderstanding of our infinite potential. For we all are perfection encapsulated in the divine mind waiting to unravel. Everything necessary for our success is already encoded within us; however, the access code lies in our understanding of our oneness with the Infinite. Charles Haanel, in his book, *The Master Key System*, put it this way: we must *be*, before we can *do*, and we can *do*, only to the extent of what we *are*, and what we *are* depends on what we *think*.

The perception of who we really are is what determines to what extent we succeed in life. It is up to us, therefore, to wake up to the reality of our true selves. For we are not just mere mortals, but divinity in manifestation, we carry infinite potential within us; we have infinite strength and wisdom. And, as we read in the scriptures, "as he is, so are we in this world,"[1] we are one with the infinite. Therefore, all things are subject to us, no matter what condition we find ourselves in, no matter what circumstances encompass us, no matter what situation befalls us. We can transcend all, knowing that with God, "all things are possible."[2] And ye are gods."[3]

Circumstances can compel us to forget our innate qualities, but we all have supernatural powers. Otherwise, how can you explain intuition? Where do ideas come from? Who can unravel the mystery behind courage? We all have limitless potential; this is the reason we need to look within to find that divine mind, that higher self, that infinite soul.

Until we make the decision to search and find our true selves, unless we connect ourselves to our divine nature, we will suffer for a very long time. And, as the scripture reminds us, "Ye are gods; and all of you are children of the most high. But ye shall die like men, and fall like one of the princes."[4] In other words, our ignorance will impede our success; it will derail our plans and trump our aspirations.

So, I implore you, my friends, to rouse the God consciousness within you; see yourself as a victor, a winner, a champion. Push aside those thoughts that belittle you and take a stand among the greats in history.

It is time to rise up and connect with that source that powers your existence, it is time to live up to your full potential, it is time to exhibit those innate qualities with which you have been endowed. Oh, common man, put your fear and doubt behind and face your future with confidence, knowing that you cannot fail, because that which powers your existence is the same that created the universe. When you understand and acknowledge that the infinite lives and dwells within you, tell me, who or what can hold you back? Is it hunger or pain, is it sorrow or sickness, is it poverty or death? No, in all these things, we are more than conquerors through him that loves us[5] and that dwells within us.

There's so much within you, so hang in there, because the best is yet to come. There's often a light at the end of the tunnel, but even when there's none, you can light a candle. So, don't give up, don't lose hope, it's not over until you say so.

BE PATIENT…THE BEST WILL APPEAR

*M*arie Corelli, in her book, *A Romance of Two Worlds*, wrote: "It is useless for you to consider the reason for this, or the meaning of that. Take things as they come in due order: one circumstance explains the other, and everything is always for the best."

Many times we break down and cry, blaming people, circumstances, and situations for our misfortunes, but our unfolding lies in the agitations resulting from our problems and challenges. Ask the oyster how she makes such beautiful pearls as she contends with irritating sands in her shell, or listen to the butterfly as she recounts her frightening ordeal in the dark chambers of her cocoon prior to her colourful emergence. People admire beauty, success, and achievements, forgetting there was a period of gestation, a period of silence, a period of loneliness and isolation.

With every mountain comes a valley, before a rise there is always a base, for a new life to emerge, there must be a dark period of conception. So, embrace your transition with equanimity, because the discomfort you feel in this moment cannot be compared to the greatness lying ahead.

I know you are going through a harrowing experience and I am in no way undermining your pain, but I am assuring you that this challenge, this pain, this frustration lays the stepping stones to the best part of your life. There is no better time than this moment; there is no better future, no better opportunity. This is a new moment; this challenge marks your new beginning, your unfolding, your emergence ... your best life starts now.

Sometimes it feels like life has put us in boxes – boxes of lack and limitation, boxes of suffering and pain, boxes of poverty and frustration. You never chose these predicaments, it is not your desire to be poor or to have a terminal illness or to be subjected to discomfort, therefore you have an option; you have the option to choose a better life, you have the option to define what you really want to be. So, hold your head up high and exercise your divine potential; turn within and tap into the infinite spirit, and through God's wisdom, knowledge, and power you will achieve all your dreams, goals, and aspirations.

I know this to be true because I have been through this journey; I have experienced suffering, I have been through pain, I know what it is to be poor, I know hunger and privation. But through these experiences, through my challenges, through my pains, I found the source of my strength. I found the great "I am" that dwells within me, I found a way to meet my challenges. You've got to understand that with suffering comes a transformation that leads to an evolution that reveals the divine person that lives and dwells within you.

The Apostle Paul corroborated this thought in Romans 5:3-5; he wrote, "we glory in tribulations also: knowing that tribulation worketh patience, and patience experience, and experience hope: and hope maketh not ashamed."[1] We are not ashamed of this hope because it is a guaranteed hope, a hope that has substance, a hope that has promise, a hope that speaks of better things for now and in the future.

So, let your heart not be troubled, my friend; be bold, be strong, have faith in the divine and in yourself. Trust the infinite spirit or the divine mind or Allah or God or whatever names you may choose to call the Absolute. It doesn't matter what you call it, it's one and the same God; he lives and dwells within you, and his ultimate purpose is to see you succeed, flourish, and excel. In the Holy Scriptures he declared that he will never leave you nor forsake you.[2] He is faithful to his promises and I am certain he will not let you down, because what he has done for one he can do for another; he did it for me, he can do it for you.

There is no need to cry, oh ... no need to frown, because your help is right here within you; and just as he had promised, he is more than willing to do abundantly all that you may ask or think.[3] The divine mind can be trusted, so turn within, quiet your mind in meditation and let the divine flood your affairs with his presence.

THIS IS YOUR NEW MOMENT

I see you wasting away, hesitating, getting involved in things you should not be involved in. Are you living that perfect life, the life you've always dreamed of?

Just the other day, I heard you belittling yourself, under-mining your special gifts and talent. What a shame, because I had looked up to you when we were much younger. You see, just because some fellow on the spur of the moment made some silly remarks about your talent does not necessarily mean that you are a failure; let him run his mouth as much as he wants, that does not change anything about you. I know you like nobody else does, I see your skills and talents. You are resilient and intelligent, you always have a new perspective and unique ideas, you are the epitome of thinking outside the box. People who misjudge you don't have any idea about who you really are, you are a creative genius. You are different, your ideas are different, your mindset is different, that is what makes you unique. If you persevere in your lateral thinking, if you pursue your unique ideas, if you dare to do things differently, the world will be at your feet.

Don't take criticism to heart. It is easier to criticize than to create. The uneducated mind finds it easy to criticize. You are a person with a purpose, a being with a specific plan to fulfil, a mission, and the one who sent you has your back. Can a man be sent to light a fire without a match, can you catch a fish from the river without a pair of hands, and can you see the world without your eyes. My friend, he who sent you will not leave you stranded; everything you need to succeed has already been provided. So be confident, do that which you have been sent to do. Your skills and talents are your tools, your passion and desires are your mandates, so go forth and shine, because you are destined to win. Do not listen to naysayers; shut your eyes and ears to errant thoughts and negative ideas. Focus on your plans until they crystallise. If in the heat of the moment your mind falters and your dreams become blurry, take a moment and bow your head and talk to the one who sent you. I promise, He will surely lead you to the light, and everything will turn out right.

Don't look back at your past; the past has no significance with your present moment. Those experiences you went through had a purpose, and that purpose was to clarify your ideas and plans. The past was therefore useful and you can use it to build the present. Yes, you did mess up in time past. Yes, you did make some mistakes. Yes, you did some shameful stuff. But that was in the past. This is a new moment, a new moment with a renewed personality, a new moment where everything is brand new. You ought to be proud that you are a survivor; you ought to be proud that you won some of the battles you fought. You ought to be proud that even though you were humiliated by past mistakes, you are still standing, you still have life, and you have another opportunity. You have a second chance to make up for your past errors. So, hold your head up high; wear your scars with pride because they are the signs of a veteran, scars are the signs of a great fighter, a warrior and a hero.

Your past experiences laid a foundation for the resilient man that you are today. So, don't listen to what people may say or to the negative thoughts in your head. You are the best in the things you do; hold your head up high, tell yourself time and again that you are the best that can ever be, tell yourself that you can make it, tell yourself that you can succeed.

Focus on the things you want to achieve, never let your goals depart from your sight. Hang on to that dream, that idea, that vision. It will take time, but in a short time it will manifest. Tough times never last; only tough people do, so hang in there and remind yourself time and time again that:

If anyone is ever going to succeed, it's got to be you.

If anyone is ever going to make it through these hard times, it's got to be you.

If anyone is ever going to walk through this dark lonely night safely, it's got to be you.

Don't forget who you are, you are not just another human. You are an emanation of the divine; for you, nothing is impossible. If your heart feels faint and your dreams begin to falter, turn within to seek guidance from the one who sent you; he lives and dwells within you, he has begun a good work in you and he will perfect it. He will see you through to the end. The battle is not yours, it is his, the one who sent you. Though the world is full of trials and tribulations, he reassured you that you will overcome. So, walk in this confidence, talk in this confidence, think in this confidence, because he will never leave you, nor will he forsake you.

STRONGER THAN YOU KNOW

I stopped and stared
Looking up for help with despair
Hope is not near
My heart was filled with fear
I sought answers
All I saw was darkness
Then I thought of an exit
I just can't take it any more
I heard a faint sound
My heart skipped a beat
Wondering what was going on
Just then I heard him speak
T'was the voice of the familiar stranger
He said listen
This will soon fade away
Just like other things that once bothered you
Nothing ever stays the same
Remember times that were far worse than these
Yet you came through

What cannot kill you
Will only make you strong
Because soon the sun will rise again
And your tomorrow
Will be greater than your yesterday
Therefore be strong
And know that you will overcome this
So there I was
Standing in the rain
I flicked a tear from the corner of my eye
With new resolve
I resumed my walk in the cold rain
Even though I was overwhelmed with despair
I put a smile on my weary lips
Because I now have a knowing
The ONE was, is, and will always be with me
Now I know that I am more than a man
I carry divinity within me
The universe lies at my feet
Waiting to bid my command
I am a co-creator with the infinite
I am one with the first cause
Effects are my manipulations
My desires will eventually come to be
I laughed out loud.
What was I thinking?
I should have known this long ago!
Then I heard him speak again
Your strength comes from within
There is no battle you can't win
You are one with the universe
And the universe is one with you
And just so you know

That you are braver than you think
And stronger than you know
The world is at your feet
Your freedom comes with your knowing
You are more than who you think you are

REASONS TO LOVE

We give what we get
We get what we give
Close your eyes and look within
Can`t you see that bright light burning?
There'll always be a reason to love
Even when all seems to be lost and gone
Brush off hate
Give love one more try
You'll be surprised
You still have so much more to give
All is not lost
Trust is not gone
There's always a second chance to make it right
Because when all else fails
Love never fails
Love knows no colour
But it does have eyes because it can see
Love knows no status, no titles, and no classes
It does not separate or segregate
Love is perfect when it's pure

So warm when it's from the heart
Love is so simple,
Everyone knows it
The language so easy
Even children could speak it
The simplest gift to give
Is to love one another
Give a smile
You get a smile in return
A little love given
Begat so much more in return
The world is such a small place
A little love is all it takes
To make it spin around
A little trust works wonders
There's no difference between us
We all came from the same source
Why don't we let a little love show?
Because everyone loves to be loved
Believe in love
Believe in God
Believe there is good in every man
What's wrong with a little hope?
A hope that someday
Men could change
Good will always come
To those who give their hearts to love
Because when all else fails
Love never fails
There's beauty in purity of heart
We attract the things we pay attention to
What if the whole world
Chose to give a little attention to love
What a big difference that would make

MORE THAN JUST A MAN

Please don't take it to heart
For in their limitation of knowledge they did speak
It was meant in good faith
Because they don't really know who they are
But we know who we are
We are the new creatures
Spoken of by the prophets of old
But now is the time of fulfilling
Our identity is about to be revealed
You doubt your existence
Yet wonder where you'll go when you die
Everyone is guilty
Searching for our origin should be a priority
Instead we abandoned this task for the pursuit of wealth
Alas, in our dying moment
We make feeble efforts to know where we were going
But then it's way too late
So we bequeath this responsibility to the next generation
Who already are necks deep in the same pursuit
Isn't it foolish that we refuse to think

But rather buy stupidity from familiar sources
We are not just flesh and blood
We are not just living beings
We are not just people
Struggling to make a living
We are not just spirit, soul, and bodies
We are source energy
Expressing itself through flesh
We are more than just human
Has it not been written in your books?
Have your teachers not told you so?
You don't belong here
You are here only for the joy of the experience
Your passion is your purpose
Your dream is your reality
Through the windows of your mind you create your existence
So, in the throes of your struggle
You find yourself in doubt of your strength
Take a deep breath and listen
He is always there to lead the way
Quiet your spirit
When everything seems to go wrong
For within you is the power to change all things
Listen, your Earth hangs in space
Suspended by nothing
Your heart has never stopped beating
Since you were born
If these facts never prove the omnipotent power
That exists within you
I wonder what will

PEACE

Peace, quiet, and serenity
Feeling close to the "I" within
I and the universe are one
Peace, quiet, and serenity
This broader knowing's setting me free
To experience the beauty of the world within
I feel the morning sun on my face
My spirit stirred
I can tell the dawn is coming
Because I feel love in my heart
And a song on my lips
I sense the touch of the divine
Oh, there's no better place to be
Than this place of peace
T'was getting brighter and brighter
As the sun slipped above the shadows of the night
I felt a whimsical smile on my lips
And a voice telling me
Everything was going to be good
Oh, it's going to be a good day

Surely it's going to be a great day
Nothing can be much better
Than to live this joyful exuberance called life
And to know that I am loved by the infinite
There is nothing I cannot do, be, or have
Because I am a manifestation of the infinite
Knowing this is the peace
That is embedded in serenity
Yes, this is the peace; I love this place of peace.

RAW POWER

Within everyman
Lies a Power that is hidden
You may call it God
You may call it Lord
Whatever name you call it
It's the raw omnipotent power
Of the infinite that man has
Revered and feared since time began
We are the creators of our life experience
Every one of us is supernatural
But ignorance has made a mockery of who we really are
For within us lies a force that can change worlds
So wake up to your reality
A reality of possibilities
Because you are not just men
Ye are Gods

SECTION II
SPIRITUALITY

This section introduces you to super consciousness, the one factor that makes your human experience metaphysical. A testament of the Divine will unravel as you delve deeply into each new page, thus culminating in your unfoldment into the super consciousness.

PRELUDE: THE SUPERHUMAN WITHIN THE HUMAN

*T*here is a higher consciousness within every man. Most religions call this consciousness God, but the name God has become so generic that it is laden with misconceptions that erode its true value. Because of these misconceptions, several authors and teachers have opted for alternative names for God. This makes some sense because when people hear you say "God," they tend to tune out. They assume they know what you are about to discuss and everyone seems to think they are an expert on that topic. Therefore, to bring a message home, it is crucial to use a different name for it, especially when you want to communicate new knowledge or information.

In *"the Master Key System"* Charles Haanel referred to this consciousness as the Infinite "I" or Universal Energy. Florence Scovel Shinn, in her book *The Game of Life and How to Play It*, calls it the "Christ within" or the "infinite spirit" or the "Super-conscious." Esther and Jerry Hicks in *The Astonishing Power of Emotions* called it "Inner Being or Non-Physical Source Energy." In this book I have used terms such as the Superconscious, the

Omnipotent, The Divine, and The Infinite, as well as God, as these words are all associated with a higher consciousness.

Motivational teachings all refer to a higher power. Usually the teachings suggest that this higher power dwells within man and that activation or connection with this power can transform man from the natural to the supernatural. You probably know someone who has met with this power. Things were not working out for this person, and the situation seemed hopeless. However, when this person read a certain book or heard a certain message, he or she was inspired and acted on the information received, and in this way the life of this person was transformed. Where did this transforming power come from? How did this happen?

Man is not just a biological entity, he is a super being who can create and transform situations. Every man is a manifestation of the infinite; we are a part of the universal consciousness or "superconsciousness. And at the same time we have the ability to function remotely. Like a machine that draws remote power from the main source but switches to its stored energy when the main source of power is shut down, man can function with his store of autonomous energy. Now, man can chose never to connect with the main energy source (such a choice is called "free will") and chose to remain autonomous, but how far can we go? Not very far. Humanity tends to favor the remote power source. He has become used to it, because it takes less effort tapping into his autonomous energy. He thinks that is how it ought to be. But this is not true.

If connecting with the divine brings out the superhuman within man, then why is he avoiding this awesome power? Why is he disbelieving of his original self? It's amusing that a man, miserable and poor, cannot accept the fact that he is a dual personality and that the unseen part of him is the reality, and that it is more powerful than the physical source because it has no physical limitation. Connection with the divine makes a man part of the force that created his physical self, and he is one and same with the infinite as a whole is the sum of all the parts.

Rather, a man trusts his government and his employers who tell him that hard work is the secret of success. Four generations have been toiling to no avail. His great grandfather toiled till he died, his father and grandfather went through life the same way. All he has ever known is labor, hard labor, and the little money he has made makes him think he is doing well because he sees other folks who are less fortunate. He works Monday to Sunday without one moment to spend in solitude, to be in touch with his divine self. They told him, "a belief in a higher consciousness or God is for ignorant poor folks." His life is full of errors and misfortunes, yet that indication has not roused him to get connected to his divine self.

The unfortunate thing for this poor working human is that his boss spends lots of time with his divine self in meditation and self-introspective thoughts. The boss needs his workers to keep his business going, and the only way to ensure that, is to discourage them from communing with the infinite. So he gives his workers more money and tells them that God does not exist, and to further ensure that his workers will not find their divine selves, he offers to pay them double for every weekend they spend at work. Foolish as he is, the man rejoices whenever he is asked to work on a weekend because he gets overtime pay. Meanwhile, his boss rejoices because he has found a mule that will till his land on Sunday while he is busy communing with his higher consciousness.

Johann Wolfgang Von Goethe said, "none are more hopelessly enslaved than those who falsely believe they are free." Your government tells you that it's the best government in the world and you are fortunate to be a part of this great system, yet you struggle every day to make ends meet. You can't cease to work for one day for fear of bills catching up with you, even in your retirement you are still paying bills. You have been toiling since you were 16 now you are 60, there seems to be no end. Does this not tell you that something must be wrong somewhere? Shouldn't there be more to life than all these struggles? What a fool you are to have believed in man instead of trusting in the infinite; you bought their lies when they told you not to believe in God. Although I can exonerate you from this blame, that does not take away from the consequences of your actions. My exoneration is based on the fact that you had a misconception of who God really is. They told you he is in Heaven enshrouded in some clouds and that he watches over you from above. But when you were in trouble he never showed up. They say "Oh, go to a place of worship, you'll surely find him there." You go there and your experience with those who are considered Holy is horrifying. You wanted real answers to your real life problems, instead you were told to have hope. "What hope?" you asked, wasn't he (God) supposed to be there when you called? Especially when you went to his house of worship? There and then you drew your conclusion that God didn't exist! So I'll say you are damn right, "that God" doesn't exist!

Now I don't know about Heaven where a thousand angels sing day after day, neither do I know about the afterlife; but the one thing I do know is that there is a consciousness that lies within man which some may call God. This consciousness is all knowing. Those who have this consciousness know all they need to know when they quiet themselves in meditation. This consciousness is all powerful, as he infuses power into those who are connected with him when they feel discouraged and helpless. This consciousness is everywhere and in everything, which explains the interconnectivity of all life forms. Every day is a journey and every moment is a new experience. This is the God that I know and this is what the scriptures told me. The scripture says "I and my father are one"[1]. "We dwell in him, and he in us"[2]; I am the physical manifestation of the infinite. "As he is, so are we in this world"[3] for we function through his breath."

The breath of the superconscious in man is what we call "life." Man and God are one.

Man must understand that he is not just flesh and blood. He thinks and the thoughts he thinks manifest into real life experiences. From his dreams and aspirations to his greatest fears, they manifest according to the thoughts he holds in his consciousness. In order to shape his life and create a pleasant future experience, man must erase that basic human concept that he can function remotely. He should strive to get connected and spend more time with the infinite, and this is the antidote for every challenge in life. There are none so hopeless as they who believe there is no God; worse still, there are none so ignorant as they who think God dwells outside the human body. To believe that God dwells within is like an electrically charged high voltage wire- you are unstoppable.

If the source of all that we can ever have or need dwells within us, why isn't everyone having the perfect life that they want? Two things are responsible for this, the first is the level of individual consciousness of the infinite that dwells within, the second is the kind of thoughts they hold in their consciousness. Man has been given a free will to use his thoughts to create whatever experience he wants, so the nature of your thoughts creates the experiences you meet in life. *Knowing thoughts are dynamic, how do you hold thoughts that create good life experiences?* The answer to this question can be found in the principles outlined in the subsequent pages. You must understand that through thoughts, we bring the things we own to ourselves. Having the knowledge and understanding of how thought works is essential in the manifestation of your desire, be it health, wealth, or love. Certain things will hijack your thoughts putting stumbling blocks every step of the way, but understanding and mastering the tools provided in this book will go a long way in harnessing your thoughts and thus bring manifestation to your desire easily and quickly. You are advised to thoroughly read and understand these principles to obtain a clear understanding of the message therein. The truth of these facts has motivated me to put them in this book.

There is an ancient saying that when the student is ready the teacher will appear. You were ready, that is why you found this book, therefore, keep the knowledge you will find within these pages to yourself. Only those who desire new knowledge seek it and find it.

These teachings have existed for a long time and only those who earnestly desire to learn put them to work. Man likes to be deceived and he loves his ignorance. To this end, Marie Corelli wrote: "The Eastern philosophers and sages concealed much of their most profound knowledge from the multitude because they rightly recognized the limitations of narrow minds and prejudiced opinions. What the fool cannot learn he laughs at, thinking that by his laughter he shows superiority instead of latent idiocy".

Let wisdom come to those who seek and the lips of the wise be sealed to the ignorant and fools.

You are at the threshold of life, transforming wisdom, be smart with the knowledge you now possess.

FORGIVENESS

"Forgiveness is like a rose that rises to bless the foot that crushed it with a scent." To me, this statement encapsulates in its entirety the definition of forgiveness. This is the most humbling statement I've ever known. Take a moment and think about this and relate it to all the bitter experiences in your life. Do you think you can help that man who crushed your spirit, that guy who stole from you or that woman who messed up your love life? When we quantify our life experiences and relate them to our current condition, nobody wants to be taken for a ride, and we all would rightly say, "Once beaten twice shy," but does that really apply to "forgiveness"? Maybe it's time to take another look at the word.

In recent years, science has shown that un-forgiveness can contribute to many illnesses. This is not news to metaphysical students. There is an ancient saying that "The only things we ever keep are what we give away." The man who wants love is the one that gives love away, if you want peace you've got to give it out first. If you want to enjoy peace of mind, then you must forgive. There is no shortcut in the laws of nature.

Florence Scovell Shinn taught in her book *The Game of Life and How to Play It* that "the fear of the lord (Law) is the beginning of wisdom." If we could understand spiritual laws, many of our problems would not exist. For instance if you send out a thought of hate to someone, you will get hate in return; if you give love you will get love in return. This law is as real as the law of gravity. So why don't we pay attention to spiritual laws despite their obvious and consistent consequences in our lives?

The universe is one and we are all part of the infinite; no one can live in isolation of universal laws. The whole is the infinite and we are the parts. Because the whole is the sum of the parts, we are all part of the infinite. Therefore, if I hate my neighbor, and my neighbor is a part of the whole, I hate a part of me. Also, if we look at what the scriptures says, "Whatsoever you give you will receive"[1] the circle must come to completion, you will definitely reap the effect of what you sow. You may have seen the effect of such examples, but you have chosen to ignore them. Raymond Charles Baker said, "All forgiveness is self-forgiveness." It's all for your own good! Jesus Christ also taught that we should love our neighbors as we love ourselves. This may seem like a tough cookie, but the truth is, we are actually practicing self-love when we love others unconditionally. Your ability to see the world as you see yourself and relate to it as you relate to yourself is the antidote for hate. As we are constantly sending vibrations to our world through our thoughts and words, these create our daily life experiences. Whatever consciousness we carry will always be reflected in our world; when we create a consciousness of love and harmony, we attract similar effects. The perception of our world is a direct reflection of our thoughts; if we perceive the world to be hateful, unfair, and partial, we will meet hateful, unfair, and partial people in our conscious world. "As is within so is without, our seed thoughts in no time yield its fruits." If your thought dwells on hate, un-forgiveness, and anger, you will definitely meet hateful, unforgiving, and angry people in your outer world. It's nice to bury our heads in the sand like the ostrich and pretend our daily life experiences are just coincidences, but it is stupid for one to deny the effects of our negative thoughts. Most times we address effects without looking at causes.

When you meet resistance in your outer world it is because it is in your consciousness. If you meet with evil it is because you have faith in evil, you expect evil, or you believe in evil. In the God realm or superconsciousness, there is no evil, and if the scripture says that "As he is, so are we in this world,"[2] then there is no iota of evil within us, and if there is no evil within us, where then does evil reside? Now, you may ask "what do you mean? Because even the Bible says the Devil is real."[3] You must understand that the consciousness of anything brings about its manifestation. Evil is not real, it has no principle; it's just wrong thoughts which can be righted by thinking right thoughts. It is not a natural state of man to be evil, it's just like a room in the dark, the moment you flick on the light switch darkness melts away. As darkness cannot withstand light, so it is with evil, it cannot withstand good! Whatever happens to us is a direct reflection of the thoughts we hold in our consciousness. Good thoughts will yield good results while bad thought bring about every negative consequence that they entail. There is an ancient saying that nothing happens without an on-looker. Whatever happens in our lives has a witness which is the kind of thought we held in mind at the time. We constantly carry the consciousness of our expectations with us. We will suffer until we understand that we are constantly creating pictures in our outer world through the thoughts we hold in our subconscious mind. I have seen many people go through various rituals to address an effect when the cause is just a very minor thought that has taken hold in their subconscious minds. The understanding of this principle was the underlying factor of Phineas Parkhurst Quimby's healing ministry. He understood that every disease has its root cause in wrong thinking and its effect is the physical manifestation of every kind of illness. All he needed to do was change the way the person thought, and healing ensued! Stop seeing evil in your world, there is no evil; the only devil that exists is your thought. Your perception of evil is your very own devil. On several occasions where people have said such and such a person was very un-approachable, when I met these "unapproachable" people I had a different experience. Your perception will create the situation you expect and eventually prove you right.

In summary, we must understand that the universe is one and we are a part of the universe. Therefore there are no enemies or the devil, evil is a concept of people mis-creating. The moment they realize their wrong thought processes they'll right themselves. You must understand that no one can institute an evil plan against you unless you are expecting it, and when it does occur you will know that it was your own creation because we create our realities through the thoughts we hold in our consciousness. You must remain nonresistant in spite of what you see or feel. The scriptures says "Recompense no man evil with evil"[4] because evil is a state of mind, a wrong thought process. Because it's a wrong thought process it can never hold light to the truth. Whatever you perceive becomes your reality. As Florence Scovel Shinn quoted that, "no man is your friend, no man is your enemy, all men are your teachers," we are all here to experience contrasting or challenging experiences in order to expand. We must learn the lessons of love by meeting people who will test the boundaries of our love, and when they do we must remain nonresistant. Our ability to remain undisturbed in spite of negative conditions is the key to the joyful life that lies ahead.

The law of non-resistance according to Florence Scovel Shinn, and *the law or the art of allowing* as described by Esther and Jerry Hicks, embody the same principle that Paul pronounced in Philippians 4:6, where he said, "Be anxious for nothing, but in everything by prayer and supplication with thanksgiving let your requests be made known to God.[5]" Don't struggle with situations, let go, knowing there is a higher power that is in control and knows what's best for you. And that higher power resides within you. Un-forgiveness is a burden, forgiveness frees your mind from bondage, and when your mind is free from thoughts that becloud your thinking, manifestations come easily. There have been instances where people forgave and a persistent illness disappeared almost immediately, some got a financial break-through, the list is endless. Never forget that "the only thing we ever keep are the things we give away" Just think about it, all those efforts and striving may not be the way to go, but by letting go, forgiving, blessing the situation or the people who may have hurt you, and moving on, you will be surprised at the amazing returns. And just like the rose, let go your scent of love when they crush your spirit. Never hold a grudge, love and bless all men as you go, and your path will be made smooth long before your arrival.

HOW TO FORGIVE.

I know how difficult it is to forgive, especially when you know you are not the cause of an agitation, but when you consider the benefits that accrue to you in letting go, it is way better to forgive. You must understand that the amount of energy needed to focus on a negative condition or an emotional state such as anger, hate, frustration, or jealousy is proportional to the amount of energy needed to create a new idea, develop a new business, or invent a useful product. Why waste vital energy that could result in transforming your life for good on some-thing that is not profitable? Forgiveness is a choice, just like other decisions we make daily. It is achievable and it is possible. I have been at that threshold, debating whether to let go or not to let go, and I know it takes will power to forgive or to let go of a painful experience. However, the joy and relief that comes when you forgive outweighs un-forgiveness. When you find it difficult to forgive, it's because you have been consistently reviewing the incident in your mind and reminding yourself of how painful the experience has been, or you feel you ought to teach the culprit a lesson so that he or she does not repeat the act. There is always something we want to hold on to, so, the leap from anger to forgiveness becomes almost impossible. This is what I do, and I guarantee it works consistently. Write an affirmative prayer, a positive affirmative prayer that highlights the good in those who have offended you and reinforces the love you have for them, knowing they are part of the infinite. You won't do this for long before it alters your state of mind, which in turn changes your feelings toward them. A change in feelings triggers an alteration of your environment. For instance, in the case of a marital dispute you'd say:

I bless you this day and wish you well in all you do, I know you are a manifestation of the infinite just as I am, for, we are from same source, same life, same breath. Therefore I cannot hold a grudge against you. May you find peace, favour, and blessings in all you do and may you meet with success every-where you go. I wish you the very best this day has to offer and I forgive you because I love.

You cannot repeat this affirmation for one week without being transformed if you really mean what you are saying. I want you to note that the change you wanted started with you not the other person. When we change the way we think and feel about a condition, it affects everything that surrounds us. Everyone naturally reacts to his or her environment; this reaction creates life experiences. The task for us, therefore, is to change the way we feel about a situation. If we can shift the feelings, with time our surroundings will change because our feel-ings (which are a part of our thoughts) create our current life experience. Don't expect others to change so that your world can be better, rather, change your thinking and perception, for it is your reaction that is creating your life experience.

GRATITUDE

ou feel depressed, you don't know why. You think you ought to be happy as you now have all that you ever wanted, but you are not. The fine home, the nice cars, a loving husband or wife, your job, all those things that were so exciting some time ago now seem to remind you of a deep void that you just can't fill. Life is becoming more and more meaningless in every way. You tried to fill this emptiness with activities, yet it's like a mirage, there seems to be no end in sight. I know that feeling, too, because I have been down there and I know how deep it can get when you get lost in it. It's the black hole of the mind, a place you'd rather not be. But if you ever find yourself in there, there is a way out, it's called gratitude.

You don't know what you've got till it's gone, and often we lose the things we have for lack of appreciation. We take life and all the simple things it gives us for granted. That you woke up this morning, that you are not ill or dead, that you can breathe, that you have a child, that you have a job you go to every day, that you narrowly missed a car accident. Trifle as it may seem, a grateful heart is a happy heart, and happiness opens the door to greater opportunities. Yet you would rather focus on the things you don't have or the pain that is bothering you. There's never going to be an end to this bucket list of desires, but if you appreciate the now and how far you have come, the air you breath, how bright and sunny the day is or how fresh the breeze is, appreciating even the mundane, you will be opening doors for those big opportunities you seek to come in. There is a saying that givers never lack. Why is it so? It's a simple life principle, giving attracts more opportunities to give, and when you give more you receive more so that you can give even more! The circle never stops. Gratitude is an expression of appreciation for what you have. The more gratitude you express, the more opportunities you will get to express even more gratitude. Express genuinely heartfelt appreciation in whatever condition you find yourself, it may not be the very best of what you wanted, but it is a stepping stone toward your destiny. In that way, you open the door to your most wanted desires.

One of the strongest factors in achieving a manifestation of any expectation is gratitude. You only need to observe the world around you to find that gratitude is a major ingredient in any growth process, from the annual corporate gifts exchanged by the big multinationals to the leaves that fall to the ground causing the ground to be nourished. Everything is expressing appreciation for the gift of giving; it's all a circle that brings about expansion in our universe. Gratitude is an inevitable process, if growth must occur.

People generally take gratitude for its literal meaning, that is, to show appreciation for a service rendered, which by no means is wrong. However, the benefit goes both ways, that is, for the giver and the receiver, but, the giver receives more. Gratitude comes from a heart that is full of appreciation; with thankfulness a heart that is full of gratitude expresses his gratefulness. In expressing gratitude the soul has come to a full circle, there is nothing more to add, rather, it gives from the abundance that is overflowing within. Gratitude is a satisfied heart seeking a joyful outlet, an out-pouring of love that is not inhibited or colored with any intentions, but is imbued with a joyful exhilaration and exploding vocals.

In recent research, grateful people have been found to be more extroverted, they have stronger immune systems and lower blood pressure, they are more agreeable, more open, and more conscientious, they are less angry, less depressed, less emotionally vulnerable, and often have positive emotions. If this is scientifically proven, shouldn't we practice gratitude more? Take away a man's hope and he's gone like the wind! But expressing gratitude for the moment gives an assured hope for another moment, another day, another tomorrow! Hope leads to belief; belief creates life experiences. If you really want to be frustrated and become depressed, it takes less than a few seconds. Just start a negative thought and in no time many more of same kind follows. A simple thought about what you could not complete yesterday could skyrocket into all the multiple failed attempts at other endeavors in your entire life. Don't judge yourself too harshly, celebrate yourself, celebrate every moment, life is for the living, you are not going to have this experience again, so be grateful for the life you have now and for the various attempts you have made at tackling some of your life challenges! You are a hero! Give yourself that liberty to congratulate yourself for your efforts. I have promised myself that when I die, I would have written on my tombstone: "This man Tried." For out of a naked little baby who arrived on planet Earth, lives were transformed, a family was raised, people were impacted with my messages. If not for anything else, for all these I applaud myself and I am grateful.

Happiness is a choice, the same goes for gratitude. You may choose to see the glass half full or half empty. Your decision will determine the state of your emotions. Contentment plays a key role in determining how you feel. Recently, I read in a forum that most singers were not happy with their voices when they first started singing, but after a while they got used to the sound of their voices and they blossomed. The point at which they accepted their voices was the point of their gratitude, and the reward was an opened gate of beauty, of color, of texture and harmonies they never believed existed, and then came the cheers and applause from the audience. Now, if they had remained in the throes of self-hate, nobody would ever have found them.

Accept yourself for who you are, my friends; there is beauty in everything if you apply gratitude. Take a listen to all the beautiful singers all over the world, do they sound alike? No. But do they sound beautiful? Yes, of course! No two singers sound exactly alike; each one is unique in his or her own way. For instance, Whitney Houston sounds so wonderful; now turn to Aaron Neville, you hear the voice of an angel. But I bet these people never sounded this way when they first started! Gratitude holds the key to the joy you are searching for. You get better at the things you do when you appreciate how far you have come.

It's a new day, a new life, a new moment. Celebrate everything, the Bible says, "in everything give thanks,"[1] be thankful for every circumstance. There is always some good tucked somewhere within that avalanche of trouble. A great percentage of achievers today had devastating setbacks before their success stories. Henry Ford was bankrupt, Bill Gates dropped out of Harvard, Michael Jordan couldn't make his high school basketball team; this list can be endless. So, were the circumstances surrounding these people pleasant? No. Were they happy with their situation? No. But did events eventually turn out to be good? Yes! In every adversity, a seed of success is embedded.

Many times our gratitude is obliterated when we think

about what we could not achieve or have not achieved. The first line in the 3rd stanza of Johnson Oatman Jr.'s song, *Count your blessings*, says, "When you look at others with their lands and gold ..." Now wait a minute, he said "others" – not what you have but what others have. In comparing yourself with others you lose the joy and excitement of what you already have! Theodore Roosevelt, the 26th president of the United States, said, "Comparison is the thief of joy."

There are no two people born at the same time from the same woman. We all came here through that portal one at a time; you are not here to compete with anybody. If anything, you ought to compare yourself with yourself, compare yourself with your goals, with your dreams, and with your aspirations, see how far you have come and how much more you need to accomplish! Paul, writing to the Galatians in chapter 6:4 said, "But let every man put to the proof his own work, and then shall he have rejoicing in him alone, and not in another." Celebrate yourself! Dwelling on lack and inadequacy takes away from the joy of thankfulness and gratitude. The cure for sleeplessness, frustration, anger, jealousy, hatred, is embedded in gratitude. Stay focused on that task; however, be sure that it is your calling, don't go hiding in some mediocre job and say you are fulfilling your destiny. We are all meant first off, to be happy, and that is the ultimate goal for every man, it is happiness that attracts all other good things, including wealth. People see success and applaud, and then everybody wants to be like the successful person. People seem to forget that there was a gestation period for the successful man. I know a musician who in his early years was in lack, he couldn't even pay his bus fare, often, you would find him walking down the street with his beat up shoes. But he was always a happy and nice fellow. He was grateful and contented in his current predicament, but he never let his vision slip away from him, he continuously worked hard at his craft. Today he is a millionaire, nobody remembers the young man that had one pair of jeans and worn out shoes.

At every moment in your life be thankful, no matter how bad a situation is, just be thankful knowing that the infinite one is always there when everything seems absolutely hopeless. For even in the midst of the rubble and dirt, a piece of glass catches a ray of sun and reflects a glow that obliterates its ugly surroundings. A thankful heart may see and feel pain but will never dwell therein. No matter what you are going through, know that God, the infinite spirit, the superconscious, the source energy, whatever name you want to call it, is always there with you. Donna Summer, in her song titled *Break Away*, sings, "forget about the bad times, remember all the good times, hold your head up high and break away." Focus on what is good and in no time everything will ease out.

In gratitude, you appreciate how far you have come and you are thankful. Gratitude births more things to be thankful for, just as ingratitude leads to more depressive thoughts. When you are overwhelmed with depressive thoughts, you can hardly see in that darkness, but if you start with little things you are grateful for, the simple things, the insignificant, they sort of buildup. Gratitude brings healing and causes us to look inside instead of looking outside. In looking within, those little things that seem insignificant become magnified. Teach your heart to be quiet. The modern way of life gives us few opportunities to have introverted reflections; it's always go-get, grab-run. People are always asking for more, not taking into account how much they already have. For a moment, focus on what you already have and forget about what you lack. This is the moment that will resolve all the unsolved problems. The moment of gratitude humbles us and causes us to feel close to the infinite. A sense of appreciation feels warm, like being wrapped up in a warm blanket on a cold winter morning, a feeling you don't want to hurry out from. It is a deliberate choice, we choose to see the world the way it is and appreciate it for the goodness and the bumps. The scripture that says *"all things work together for good"*[2] feels so true when you come into the place of gratitude. There is no negative experience in this life that does not have a positive side. You may not see it when the heat of the trouble is on, but after a while it will unravel. Gratitude brings us in close consciousness with the divine, we radiate joy, we find it easier to love and be loved, and the world becomes a happier and better place. Gratitude begets more gratitude, it is a chain link; gratitude has a tendency to pull out more good things to be grateful for. Look around you, there is so much to be grateful for. Take a moment and write down just one thing that you are grateful for, right now. Stop everything you are doing and really consider what you are most grateful for. Once noted, consider this one thing when you wake up every morning, think about it for five minutes before starting your day. I promise you, you will be bouncing through your day with exuberance because you have a reason to live, and because you have a reason to live, you now have a reason to be grateful, and grateful people make happy and successful people.

A GRATITUDE PRAYER

©2015 Kc O'Kerry
I am grateful for this day
For the fact that I am alive
I am grateful for this journey called life
And how far I have come
I am grateful for my health
And because I have faith and hope, it can only get better
I am grateful for my family
And how we complement each other in our growth process
I am grateful that I have a child
And for the joy and laughter she brings to my life

I am grateful for today
And for all that I can do at this moment
I am grateful for the future
And for the hope that things will always get better
I am grateful that I have God
The source of all that I have and ever hope to have
For all these and more, I am grateful

AFFIRMATION

*A*ffirmations are positive statements that re-enforce positive thoughts and challenge and override negative thoughts. A well-crafted affirmation provides a strong image for the subconscious mind to latch on to, and a repetitive application of an affirmation births an expectation in real time. Affirmations are audible versions of a visual held in the mind, and this visual could be an object or a life experience. An affirmation reinforces the consciousness of a desire and strengthens a belief in its manifestation.

Words are means to communicate; however, they also contain vibratory power. The vibratory effects of words are immeasurable. Words can stir up emotions wherewith a grown man can cry, a mob also can be mobilized. Understanding the vibratory power of words and knowing how to use them separates the Super humans from the humans.

What you believe affects your life experience. Belief is built up over time and experience. For instance, an event in your life causes a belief, and further events can strengthen that belief. After many such events, the belief becomes so strong that it is transformed to a real life experience.

Now a manifestation or a life experience occurs by having faith in an expectation or by holding the object of your desire consistently in mind. A thought held in mind is repetitive, in other words your mind consistently plays over and over again what you are expecting. So when you are affirming, you are creating a situation deliberately to suite your expectation. Our words and thoughts are very powerful because they carry vibratory powers that create life experiences. Humans are vibrational beings; the extent to which we deliberately create our vibratory experience is based on our consciousness of our vibratory power, and as we know, power comes through consciousness. Affirmations are intentional positive vibrations. Whether we vibrate through our thoughts or through our voices, our daily life experiences are the results of such vibrations.

Affirmation makes a positive demand on a desire, and the consistent repetition of an affirmation creates a conscious possibility, otherwise known as a belief. A belief quickly moves to the realm of expectation, now what you are expecting is no longer a hope, it's no longer a "how," it is a "when."

Affirmations work best when mixed with a strong desire or a dire need. For instance, a challenge in your pathway creates the desire for a change; the speed with which this change occurs is proportional to how much or how strongly you desire this change. The propelling power or factor that creates this change is thought. By using affirmation, you seed the thought of your expectation, and by holding it in mind through repetitive affirmation, your expectation objectifies.

Things that have evidence or proof tend to manifest more quickly than things that have never been seen or heard. The reason is that the mind knows it has been done before; therefore, it can be done again. This is why feats are easily repeated in sports and other endeavors engaged in by man.

For instance, if you have a 9 am to 5 pm job that gives you a reasonable amount of income, you may never bother with affirming to get rich, as this job meets almost all your basic needs. Now, assume you migrate to a new country where you have been told that you can be an instant millionaire if you ever get there. On arrival, you may not experience the riches instantly, in fact, for the first six months, your standard of living may drop below the standard you knew in your home country. Yet you have high hopes, you have a conviction, a belief that there is a possibility of attaining maximum wealth. You have seen that many who arrived just like you with nothing, with time have become successful. Therefore, you will be consistently hopeful because you have a proof of your belief and you are convinced that what you desire is attainable. As the scripture says: "faith is the substance of things hoped for, the evidence of things not seen,"[1] the people around you are the evidence, you don't need any further proof, and your eyes have seen what your ears have heard! So believing in evidence you already have is easy, therefore, its manifestation is quicker.

So do we need to have proof before believing that our expectations are possible? Absolutely Not! This is where the power of affirmation comes in. Affirmation creates this belief. In creating an effective affirmation we must imitate how the mind responds to familiar things, by using associations. Associating words and situations with your affirmation helps the mind create a belief. But this belief must be backed with a strong desire. Needing something and wanting something are two separate platforms. In the wanting, you will look for the reason for wanting it. But if you need something, nothing stands in your way; you don't need to explain to anybody the reason for needing it. You have to have what you need! A need tears down every barrier. The key ingredient in making a manifestation through an affirmation is "A strong desire" A NEED.

In the early 1990's I joined a dogmatic Christian movement. Back then, we were told to be careful with our words. We were told that our words were potent as they contain the manifested power of God and that whatever we say becomes real. With time, we did witness some manifestations, but most of the time we didn't. It took several years before I understood the science behind the inconsistencies. The truth was that we were offering stronger vibrations for the things we feared than for the things we wanted. The strongest vibrations can manifest in reality irrespective of your expectation. Most of the time when we pray, we pray in fear of an impending doom, so while petitioning our God for protection, we feel the fear of the danger lurking behind, and the vibration we offer is of fear and not of confidence in an all-powerful God who is willing and ready to save us.

In my earlier Christian faith experiences, most of our prayers were petitions. We begged God for healing, wealth, and health and ended our prayers with "if it is thy will, oh God," let me have such and such thing, or we would say "Oh God, let your will be done." This last part was the stumbling block that caused delayed results or no results at all in our petitions. The simple reason for this was because these statements negated the initial request. It is hopelessness and despair against desperation and fear; nothing can ever come out of that! It's like receiving an employment offer. The owner of the business says to you "hey, skip the interview process, just come straight to my office, and pick up your letter of employment." Instead, you ignore his offer and prepare for a job interview for a job that has already been offered to you, how ridiculous!

I've heard a few people say affirmations don't work, I'd say these people are absolutely right! Affirmations don't work for those who don't believe in them! The reason for this is that whatever you believe manifests in your reality. If you don't see yourself becoming rich, you can never get rich. God told Abraham, "For all the land which thou seest, to thee will I give it[2]" You will have only what you envision!

A thought held in mind, especially a thought about something you really want, is repetitive, you are constantly musing about it until its final execution. The repetitiveness is the affirmation, you are unconsciously agreeing with the infinite that, this is what I want, this is what I want, this is what I want, and because you held it in mind for so long in time, it objectifies! Just think for a moment, is there anything you have ever wanted that you did not first think about before you got it? For instance, if you are afraid of a situation, it will play in your mind over and over again, and most times the things you are afraid of manifest in your life quickly. Why is this so? The reason is that you are affirming to the universe that what you don't want is what you want, you are holding that image of what you don't want in your mind! In this process you are not a deliberate creator, you are creating by default. You must take charge of your life by deliberately choosing your thoughts. Choose an affirmation that addresses the direction you want to go. Be specific in your expectation and remain focused on your expectation.

We are more than just humans, yet many people can't even think beyond the next lunch or dinner or the next pleasurable experience. We should be masters of the universe, creating how we feel or where we want to be or what we want to do. We are more than just men! For everything that we achieve in life, there is first the conception, then the belief that it is possible, and finally the manifestation. Whatever you become is first formed in your head before you become it. If you can see it in your head you most certainly can have it. Through affirmation you create your belief, your belief assures you that it is possible, and then comes the manifestation. The truth about life is that nothing is real until you bring it to manifestation. This applies to everything that has ever been invented, but it starts with a thought, and the thought crystalizes to a belief, and belief then creates the reality you see.

There are two common types of affirmation, the assertive

affirmation and the denial. From personal observation, an assertive affirmation can be used as a standalone application, because it puts forth its argument straight away. However, a denial first acknowledges the absence of a need and then follows this acknowledgement with an assertive affirmation. If a denial is not well written it just emphasizes the vacuum. That is why most denials are immediately followed by an assertive affirmation. I rarely use denials as I consider them to cause round tripping. For instance, suppose that you want to participate in a 100 meter dash. You stand in a line with the other competitors. The whistle blows and everyone else dashes forward toward the finish line. But you head off in the opposite direction to the locker room to pick up your running shoes before catching up with the others, ridiculous, right? Exactly! That is what I've found with denials. In denials you are trying to offset a situation before stating your desire, which I find to be time-wasting

I have found that denials acknowledge the absence of something that you are trying to create. But assertive affirmation goes straight to the point, stating exactly in vivid words what you want! For instance," I have used an affirmation which states: "A wedge has been placed at the door of my success and no one can shut it." The imagery in this affirmation was so strong that each time I affirm it; I can physically feel a surge of adrenaline rush through me. That is what a powerful affirmation does; it assures you of the possibility of your expectation. A repetitive application of an affirmation brings about confidence and confidence translates to belief, belief then brings the affirmation into a real life experience. Creating a great assertive affirmation is quite easy. All you have to do is look around you; there are abundant symbols or objects in your culture that represent what you are looking for!

Here is my process of creating affirmations. I think of a word in picture and then add words that describe the picture in its strongest visual terms. I'd advise you to use images that are familiar to your environment or culture; affirmations have more impact when they are based on association. The Bible is a handy tool for creating quick assertive affirmations. Below I provide samples of affirmations.

STARTING A BUSINESS

I see before me all the land; as far as I can see has been given unto me.

SUCCESS

> *I am one with the universe*
> *and the universe is one with me*
> *Let everything I touch turn to gold*
> *Because I am mystical and magical*
> *So cut me loose oh infinite one*
> *Let the rumble begin*
> *By grace in perfect ways.*

CHILD PROTECTION

> *I put a shield of protection round about my child*
> *Like the white light of Christ,*
> *She will not be moved by the circumstances*
> *In her environment,*
> *Rather she is a positive influence in her generation.*
> *Therefore be strong oh child, be strong*
> *You are the leader of the positive pack.*

JOB SEARCH

Like a dam that broke loose,
I am overwhelmed by job opportunities.
From the left to the right,
From the top to the bottom;
I am the child of the King
All things are at my command
And I must have only the best
By grace in perfect ways

JOB SEARCH

As my father made everything in abundance,
So it is with me; I am flooded with limitless opportunities,
I lack nothing that is good for my benefit.

BOLDNESS

A dead man feels no pain nor has any fears, I am one with Christ therefore I am invincible, I am immortal, I am powerful, I am the hunter not the hunted, I am the threat not the victim, let the whole world bow before me for, I carry raw powers of the omnipotent.

CONFIDENCE

"Greater is he that is in me than he that is in the world"[3]

COMFORT AND ASSURANCE THAT YOU ARE NEVER ALONE

"Even when I go through adversity, my teacher shall always be with me for with mine ears I will hear his counsel telling me this is the way, walk ye in it"[4]

TRAVELLING

"And, behold, I am with thee, and will keep thee in all places whither thou goest, and will bring thee again into this land; for I will not leave thee, until I have done that which I have spoken to thee" Genesis 28:15.

ABUNDANCE

I can feel the whirlwind of success blowing my way; I know that that which is mine is on its way to manifestation.

HARMONY

If I am what I think I am
That the infinite and I are one
And the universe is what I think it is,
That the universe is a cosmos and not chaos
Then I am in harmony with everyone and everything
That comes into my sphere of contact
Therefore let wealth and riches, fame and congenial friends
Come to me in an avalanche of abundance
By grace in perfect ways

STARTING A BUSINESS

As he calls a bird of prey from the east
And a man from a distant land to execute his counsel[5]
So it is with my business.
I call on all the resources I need, the talents, the skills and
    finances.
Everything I need is right there just when I need it
My supplies are in endless flow
by grace in perfect ways.

INTERVIEW

As a piece of metal cannot resist the pull of a magnet
So it is with my interviewer
I am irresistible and that which is mine
must be mine by grace in perfect ways.

HEALTH

As a reset button reprograms a computer to its default setting, so it is
with my body. I am renewed from within and without, I am
completely restored.

HOUSE SEARCH

As supply is met by demand, so it is with my desire for my perfect
home. I cannot be denied what is mine by divine right, therefore infi-
nite spirit, open the way for my perfect home in the perfect place with
the perfect rent, a home that is mine by divine right. I give thanks that
it manifests on time under grace in perfect ways.

FINANCES

Infinite spirit, open the way for my place of super abundance, a place of wealth immeasurable, bring me into my place of comfort and destiny where effortlessness brings about absolute and maximum wealth and affluence. I command my fortunes to come rolling in, in an avalanche of abundance by grace in perfect ways.

Note: Florence Scovel Shinn, in her book *The Game of Life and How to Play It*, explained about expectations that are manifested in perfect ways (that is, free from any karmic consequence). You don't have to covet what others have, just as there is a blade for every grass, so there is supply for every demand. What is yours will be yours and it comes perfectly fit for you, and its manifestation has to be in perfect timing.

A MORE POWERFUL TYPE OF AFFIRMATION: "GPS"—GUIDED POSITIVE SPEAK

*W*ords are thoughts expressed in sound. Often they are taken for granted because they are effortless, unless you have an oral dysfunction. That being said, the process in which words come through when we speak may not be as simple as we want to believe. Every word we speak starts with a thought. Thought is mind in motion, for mind in itself is static or inactive, but through the action of thought becomes active. So the origin of words is the mind. Mind does not come up with ideas on its own; it uses materials from the conscious, the subconscious, and the superconscious (I discussed this extensively in the chapter *"Living above Fear"*). When you hear someone speak, he is not just communicating, he is utilizing a force that transforms lives and circumstances. There is an African proverb that says: good words come from a good heart. If a man's words sound good to you, it is likely that the thoughts behind them are also good. So, what constitutes a good heart or mind? It's the kind of thought it entertains. You might ask, can anyone keep his thoughts pure? To answer this question, sit still and quiet your thoughts; keep your mind blank for five minutes without entertaining any thought. Were you able to do that? I know you couldn't. I have done this exercise with various people and the result has always been the same. Nobody can keep his or her thoughts from wandering. However, you can keep your thoughts from wandering into specific areas by supplying specific thoughts or ideas. But what if you are disturbed by a particular condition and your desire to change that condition dominates your thoughts? In such case you need to build a positive momentum through a process I call "guided positive speak" or GPS. GPS builds up a sustained vibration through the words we speak, which triggers a positive response in our bodies, which in turn gives us hope that our expectation of good will be manifested. Guided positive speak is just like driving in a bad road condition. In driver's training we are told that if your car starts skidding while driving, ease off the accelerator and gently steer your car in the direction you want to go. GPS is about easing off the pressure caused by your active thoughts which has caused resistance as you make a mental demand for a change in your condition. GPS starts slowly but gathers momentum as you continue to use positive words to describe the current unpleasant condition.

As a practitioner and strong believer in affirmation, I know that almost every negative condition can be put right with a good affirmation. However, certain conditions can distract your attention. A regular affirmation may fail when a negative thought dominates your thinking. Some of those thoughts may come as subtle questions, such as "why did she say this" or "how could he have done that?" These questions may seem harmless at first but you have probably noticed that they capture strongholds in your subconscious mind and they are bottomless as you delve in to solve the mystery behind them. This is where GPS comes into play.

For instance, I once had a suspicion about the activities of a friend. Every day I would dwell on the scope and the possibility of certain things happening. I never confronted him about these issues but often I would indulge in fantasies of having him lie or falsify some information or steal something. As I have said before, we create our life experiences through the thoughts we hold in our consciousness, therefore, my karma returned quickly. Soon my friend started spreading false information about me. I tried everything to bring peace to my heart and to the situation, to no avail. Sometimes in my quiet time while making an affirmation, my mind would wander and I'd struggle to rein it back into focus. Suddenly it dawned on me that my affirmation was generating resistance rather than effecting the changes I wanted! Normally an affirmation reinforces positive thoughts, which in turn create an expectation or a life experience. But in a situation such as mine, where the vibration of what has already gone wrong was stronger than the positive thought I was generating, a normal affirmation only fueled resistance because it reminded me of what went wrong!

The words we speak or the things we hear create vibrations which in turn influence our physical condition. Our vibrations spell out exactly how we feel and what we want and that is what the infinite responds to. When we speak or hear something exciting, our bodies vibrate, this vibration is proportional to the level of our expectation. Whatever preoccupies your mind offers the strongest vibration. In my case, even though I was making an affirmation for a positive change in my affairs, my fears were betraying me through a stronger vibration, therefore the change I expected never manifested. To correct this I needed to perform GPS to take my mind completely off the situation but at the same time reaffirm my desire in a way that it didn't generate resistance. The beauty and strength of GPS lies in the strength of the words you speak, moment by moment. You don't have to script your words, neither do you have to repeat specific words as with regular affirmations; it's about saying something positive about things that are happening around you as they come into your sphere of thought. It is a continuous flow of positive words. GPS creates a cloud of positivity around you as you speak spontaneously.

Man was designed to create his life experience through his words and thoughts. This is obvious in the way we function. No one can carry out any action without first contemplating it. We think before we take any action. Everything we do we first hold in our head or brain, fine tuning it before taking action. Does that not tell you that we are first nonphysical? As far as I know, Man is the only being who can recreate his affairs through thoughts and through the words he speaks. Everyone can do this; we see proof of our supernatural abilities every day in our daily interactions.

Creating your own GPS might initially seem awkward, since it requires you to speak spontaneously. With time it becomes easier. Below are examples of what I would say when experiencing resistance in a particular situation.

I bless this day
Bless this moment
Let there be joy
In the things I see, feel, touch, and hear
Oh I see beauty
I see love
I see joy round and about me
Oh I see possibilities
I see possibilities in my dreams coming true
I see possibilities in my aspirations
I see possibilities that I am doing well in all my affairs
This is the best day of my life and I am thankful
I am thankful that I have good health
I am thankful that only good things will come my way today
I am thankful that the infinite is my guide and help
Both in thoughts and actions
I am never alone at any time

The infinite is always with me
He tells me what to do and when to do it
He is my secret source of strength and inspiration

I may be saying the above while getting ready to leave my home for work. As I step outside my door, walking to the car, I would say:

The infinite is my defense
He protects me from incidents and accidents
There is a force field around me that shields me from harm
I am invincible
Oh my car is in perfect condition
As I drive through the streets
The roads are free from traffic
I see friendly faces
Everyone I meet today is nice to me

Till this moment, I haven't mentioned the condition that is bothering me and if you have been deeply engrossed in my flow of words, you will also notice that you are beginning to warm up to the positive words I am speaking. Every word I am speaking right now was not preplanned; I speak as the words come to my consciousness, however, I am careful that they are positive words. It is like thinking aloud, but in a guided way. The beauty of this process is that you can use it anywhere. You don't have to speak aloud for everyone to hear. Even if you are working in an office at the moment, you can be uttering under your breath:

Whatever I do, I do well
I am getting better at what I do every day
I am a very vital part of my work team
Therefore I am indispensable

Remember what I said about using only positive statements? The word "indispensable" sounds negative, even though it is a positive condition. If you take out the first two letters what do you get? – "dispensable." Stay away from words that sound negative, rather, say:

Whatever I do, I do well
I am getting better at what I do every day
I am a very vital part of my work team
My contributions are of great value
Hence my boss will continually seek my opinion
I am the best
And will always be the best

If at this point the thought of what is bothering me comes up, I will seamlessly add it to the flow of my positive thoughts. Never disrupt the momentum of joy that you have built:

I am not bothered by the circumstances surrounding me
For my father, the infinite, is in charge of all that concerns me
Everything works for my good
This situation is no different
I see good in adversity
I see joy in this challenge
Things can only get better with me
Oh I have seen it happen before
And this shall still pass away like every other condition
And I will get stronger and better at the end of the day
I am excited about my future
Because it is so bright and full of fun
These are the best times of my life
Nothing is comparable to what lies ahead
Day after day, idea after idea
I am unfolding into a better me

I am unstoppable

Again, notice the transformation in the conversation. It started with acknowledging the challenge but gradually morphed into a positive affirmation. If it were a normal affirmation, a thought such as that would weaken your confidence, but GPS uses that intrusive thought as a pivot to launch more powerful statements which take you higher in your positive states. Sometimes the statements I make while using GPS are so powerful that they stick around in my subconscious mind and they pop out like affirmations when negative conditions are trying to take hold of my thought.

Life is in the now, we have been admonished to live in the moment, for in this moment there are no crises, no worries or fears. Worries come from the past, and the future is yet to be determined, but your action at the moment will shape your now and your future. So, design your future through the words you speak now.

You can see how the challenge of a pressing negative thought can be turned around and used as an opportunity to channel a better future. The words we speak build up layers of experiences that manifest with time. Your whole life rotates around your thoughts. The words you speak and the thoughts you hold in your consciousness will determine where your future lies. Never fall into the trap of letting your thought drift like a ship without a rudder. You cannot stop your mind from straying once in a while, but you can rein it in by feeding it with specific thoughts, thus channeling harmony in your affairs. While you are at your business or doing any routine task, forge something beautiful with words and thoughts. This process keeps you from anxiety or fear or other negative emotions while at the same time creating a positive aura around you.

UNCONDITIONAL LOVE

*T*he troubles we experience in our lives were never meant to torment us or to punish us for some wrong doings; rather, they teach us lessons and bring about experiences that shape our present and our future. This is not some philosophical statement or some religious sentiment; this is a truth that has been taught by sages and teachers of ancient civilizations. In order to go through a painful experience without frustration, anger, hate, or any negative emotion, you must learn to love the pain; you must love "unconditionally."

Unconditional love requires that you extend yourself beyond your present circumstances, embracing every condition as a learning experience. What we discuss in this chapter is beyond the general definition of love, for love itself is a creative force; it is not only the passionate feeling it is generally associated with. To love is to create; the essence of loving is to put man in charge of his environment. The concept of unconditional love runs through science and almost every religion. For instance, Jesus taught "Love your enemies, do good to them that hate you, bless them that curse you and pray for them that despitefully use you."[1] In other words, extend yourself beyond your ego. In psychology, the term "cathect" means to invest emotional energy on a person or an object. It is an extension of the self beyond the ego boundaries. The Greek origin of the word cathect (Kathexis) means retention, or to hold. M. Scott Peck, MD, in his book *The Road Less Traveled*, said that in order to cathect an object, the object must first become beloved; that is, when we extend ourselves beyond the self toward an object, we become attracted to the object and we fall in love with it; then the object becomes an extension of our selves. In Buddhism we read that "Hatred is never appeased by hatred in this world. By non-hatred alone is hatred appeased." Therefore, we must love in spite of absolute negative conditions.

Irrespective of prevailing conditions, we must extend ourselves beyond the boundary of the self; this is what Christ and all the sages have emphasized in their teachings. Loving unconditionally has the benefit of creating an environment where creativity thrives. A situation does not have to be beautiful or attractive and desirable before we love unconditionally, we must love unconditionally irrespective of any prevailing situation; it is a deliberate choice. Today this concept is a lost art, as vengeance and un-forgiveness takes preeminence, bringing with it, to everyone's chagrin, consequences adequately deserved. People are often awed by the negative conditions that surround them, and tend to forget that they were the cause of these conditions.

The submissive nature of unconditional love does not necessarily make anyone a doormat; rather, it is based on the understanding that no matter what adverse condition you find yourself in, you must be open minded, forgiving, and loving. Though people or persons sometimes may be catalysts for the appearance of an adverse condition in our lives, they might not be the reason why we have such experiences; the reason might rest on our pattern of thought or the state of our mind. What is more important than the adverse condition is the experience and lessons to be learned from it. Remember that every experience that comes into your life is meant to shape you into perfection. With every incident, every man should ask himself "what am I supposed to learn from this experience?" In so doing, you will find that the focus is no longer on the imagined perpetrator but on what lessons need to be learned. There is an ancient saying that "no one is your enemy, no one is your friend, all men are your teachers."

In focusing on the lessons to be learned from an experience, two things happen. First, you lose focus on the person who supposedly was the cause of the incident that upset you, and in losing focus on that person you cease to hate him or her. Second, the law of attraction, which states that we attract things we hold in our consciousness, is short circuited. In other words, because you did not react to your current condition, the consequences that would have resulted from your action do not occur. An example of this theory is outlined below.

I once attended a course, and from all observations the lecturer, XX, disliked me. I knew the metaphysical reason for the dislike. I was holding a negative thought of XX's personality in my subconscious mind– XX had a whiny voice and I was secretly amusing myself with the whiny sound of his voice without realizing that my negative thought would generate a negative consequence in my reality.

In that course we were expected to complete a piece of work in record time. XX ensured that I did not finish my project by refusing to give approval of my work so that I can progress to the next level of assignment. Now, based on the marking criteria for the course, an unfinished project automatically qualifies for failure. After the allotted time for a project is complete, the participants must move to the next project. Participants who did not finish the previous assignment are allowed to retouch their work in their spare time. I saw a few participants do this, but when I tried to do the same, XX would tell me to stop and move on to the next project; I was flustered.

When I observed XX's behavior, initially I panicked, but a statement from the book *Your Word is Your Wand* by Florence Scovel Shinn came to mind. Scovel Shinn wrote, *"My ships come in over a calm sea, under grace in perfect ways."* I recited this phrase every time I felt agitated. Scovel Shinn also wrote: "bless the situation," "bless this person," and "never hold a grudge." I quickly recovered from my frustration and started blessing XX and the situation. I said to myself, XX is bringing to me a very valuable life lesson that will shape my future, therefore, XX is my angel and I am willing and ready to learn whatever this experience is going to bring me. I became cheerful toward XX, even smiling whenever we met. From the moment I took Scovel Shinn's advice until the end of the course, I never had a negative thought or feeling toward XX.

On the last day of the course I was handed my result. I was one mark short of the passing mark. But there was a condition. There was an exam coming up that afternoon, and if I passed that exam, it would nullify the current failure. That afternoon I was shaky and distraught. I kept muttering to myself "what have I done to XX?" "why should I deserve this treatment?" "why me?" "why should I fail after so much hard work?" Then I chided myself, saying, you are a student of *Truth*, you have learned that no man is responsible for any condition in your life; you created your current life experience through the thoughts you held in your consciousness. XX has nothing to do with this! He is just a messenger, a messenger who is here to point out a deficiency in your life! Then I asked myself, "what is this deficiency?"

Suddenly I realized that I had genuinely loved XX over the course of this agitation despite what he has done to me; in other words, I loved him unconditionally. Unconditional love? Yes! That was it; that was what I was supposed to learn from this experience! Until now, I did not know that unconditional love was practicable; but here I was, completely and totally practicing it. My lesson was complete. Even though I failed that exam, I had passed excellently a crucial test in the Life exam! With that decided, I recited my forgiveness prayer.

THE BLESSING

©2015 Kc O'Kerry

As water flows down from the mountain top
And as florets of dandelion are released into the air
I let go every feeling of anger, pain, and anxiety
I let go, I let go, I let go
As rain water drips down from the roof top
And as the wind blows ashes off the burnt woods
I let go every thought that is not serving me
Memories of pain and un-forgiveness
I let go, I let go, I let go
I am one with the universe
And the universe is one with me
I identify with all mankind
Knowing, all men are a golden link in the chain of my good
No one is my enemy, no one is my friend
All men are here for my good
Even when there is injustice on my pathway
I know it's all part of the bigger picture
That will bring me greater blessings
No matter what I see
No matter what I feel
I do not hold anyone in contempt
I forgive everyone and I let them go from my mental grip
Let every negative condition dissolve into nothingness,
Let it go, let it go, let it go

As the sun rises every morning and blesses all men with its
brightness
And as the rain falls down from the sky and causes life to
blossom
I hold my love true to all
No hate no alienation no separation
As all men are equal before the infinite
So is my heart open to all
Everyday day is a new beginning
Every morning is a fresh start
Let my love flow to all
Irrespective of who they are or what they are
Let it flow, let it flow, oh just let it flow
I salute this day with the joy of the moment
Knowing, only good is in store for me
The infinite is never too late
For he also serves those who wait
I surrender my dreams, my aspirations, my worries, and my
cares to him
Knowing, my strength comes from nonresistance
My happiness is not with any person, place, or thing
My happiness comes from the "I" that dwells within
Moods of those around me can't dictate how I feel
I feel how I want to feel, when I want to feel, how I want to feel
Therefore, I release myself into the arms of the infinite,
trusting his guidance in every moment.
I bless this day with the blessings of the infinite
Let there be peace and harmony in all my affairs
Let there be peace, let there be peace, oh let there be peace

With that said, I sat and calmly wrote the exam.

When the results came, I was one of the few students that passed! That automatically negated the previous result.

Normally humans respond only to those who show kindness

or love to them, and hate those who dislike them. In the face of a negative condition, through knowledge of unconditional love, I overcame a daunting challenge. Based on spiritual principle, XX had nothing to do with the situation even though XX was the perpetrator. Now you may ask, is XX justified for what has happened being that a divine order was carried out? In Matthew 18:7, Jesus said, "Woe unto the world because of offences! For it must needs be that offences come; but woe to that man by whom the offence cometh!" Jesus is saying here that at some point in time offences are inevitable, but woe to that man by whom the offence come. Why? Because he has started a negative process that will cascade down his future!

Nonresistance in any situation nullifies a negative consequence; a reaction offers an active vibration that ricochets. As you will come to understand, the universe only speaks and understands vibration. So when you are screaming noooo! Why meeeee!? You are offering a strong vibration, telling the universe yessssss! I want more of this stuff, I want moooore! When you are not disturbed by what you see, feel, or experience, apparently you are not offering a vibration, and everything fades out without consequence.

Now, I don't know what the infinite has in store for XX, neither should that be any concern of mine, for as far as all is concerned a divine order was carried out and XX ensured that it was carried out to the letter, and I, on the receiving end went through the experience triumphantly! We all are here in this time space reality to accomplish our life experiences, which are crucial for the evolution of the human race. The learnings are all that matters. Man must master the self, so that the self and the infinite may become one. Can you imagine what we can do if we are permanently fused with the infinite? It's mind-blowing.

Sometimes we may have an urge to fix a disturbing situation, especially with a case such as I described with XX, as I have evidence to prove my innocence. If we carry out a counter attack we may succeed, but I assure you the victory will not be as lasting and sweet as a divinely planned victory (through nonresistance). The divine victory is a clean victory, no words or blows exchanged a victory so obvious that your assailant will never consider another attack.

As I mentioned earlier, love is a creative force or a tool that is used to shape conditions and life experiences. The previous experience was about a person, the following is an instance where unconditional love redefined a situation.

When I first arrived in Canada, I got a job in a retail outlet. My tasks were to help customers load their merchandise into their cars and trucks, move trolleys that customers left carelessly in the parking lot and stack the trolleys in sheds. Now here was a man who was well educated and had had a very comfortable life in his home country, but was currently doing menial jobs. I hated every single day; there were days I just didn't want to wake up, it was like an unending nightmare. But somehow all the metaphysical principles I had learned over the years came flooding into my consciousness and I got encouraged.

Every day before heading out to work, I made affirmations; this set the tone for my day. At work, I had a song on my lips; I wore the brightest smile, and worked the hardest. I always arrived at work early and infused as much dignity as I could into my tasks. People naturally gravitated toward me like I was some kind of magnet. In fact, a couple of them came up to me and said "Hey, you don't seem to fit in here, why are you working here?" Some offered advice on how to get a better job; others offered tips on career redirection. Even my employer was impressed with my work ethic and I got several good reviews within a short time. Not very long after that, I was moved to another department, but then it was time to move to a higher paying job; a career choice that came through a tip from one of the customers I served! Note that the change I wanted came because I had a positive attitude which attracted people who were willing to help me. Even though I was angry at my circumstance, I did not direct my frustration at my job or at the customers I served.

In another instance, a lady called me on the phone, highly distressed. She said she had quarreled with her husband, and now for over a week her husband would not talk with her. I told her to calm down and I asked about the details of the matter. I found they had a disagreement over some trivial issues and had put up resistance with each other. I said, "First you must let go of every angry and ill feeling toward him, love and trust this man even though he seems to be oppressive." Then I told her to get a piece of paper and shred it into tiny pieces and blow it into the air, then I gave her this affirmation, I said "as these pieces of paper are blown into the air, so it is with this situation, let it blow away, let it blow away, let it blow away, let there be peace in my home and in all my affairs." I told her to repeat this continuously and that I also would affirm with her every day. You may ask, what is the reason for shredding the paper into pieces? Well, I have found that affirmation works fastest when associated with imageries that you easily relate to. There is nothing to the piece of paper, it just represents a physical description of an action taken, and the mind recognizes this too. After a week she called in ecstasy; she said "What did you do? What did you do? Anyway, I don't care what you did but this is magical! My husband has changed; he is now very nice to me!" I told her "I did nothing, I only affirmed along with you and your condition changed." I advised her to continue with the affirmation and to maintain her nonresistance and to refrain from anger and every negative emotion and all would remain beautiful.

So, whenever you find yourself in a negative condition, apply the unconditional love principle, love whatever it is!

Hating the situation means resistance and in resistance you get stalled. Can you now understand why you are still in that job for so long despite the fact that you just can't stand it any longer? That guy who shares your desk at work, who keeps you offended with his silly jokes and snide remarks will remain with you until you learn to love and accept him as a fellow traveler in this journey called life. You've got to love people and let them be who they want to be, you are not God's police or his chief etiquette officer. You were never appointed to tell people how best to behave because even you, your very presence, drive some people nuts! So just let others be, and you will find peace and harmony in your own little world. Hating, complaining, or avoiding negative conditions will never get you out of it; in fact it will dig you deeper into your pain. Unconditional love is the key to your freedom. Unconditional love lets you overlook a person or a situation and lets you see the reason why you are having an experience. Hate is not an option and it will never be. For a universe that is ever in motion, why would you want to hold a grudge when in reality you have already moved on? Every moment you progress toward an older you, so why would you want to hold on to a hurt that had happened in the past. Isn't it just like a car that is engaged in a gear, revving and ready to go but you are trying to hold it still? The situation before you is just a pointer to the part of you that needs to be fine-tuned! Let go the hate, anger, and jealousy, they are never beneficial, focus on the lesson that the experience is bringing, that is the reason you are going through what you are going through at the moment.

Often in life, people just want success irrespective of whatever field they find themselves in. They'd say, all that matters is the fame and wealth. They just want to have what their friends or colleagues have. What they don't realize is that; for every man or woman, there is a purpose or a real reason why they are on earth. When you find your purpose, you will excel. You will be respected, people will be grateful that you do what you do for a career. It may not bring you massive wealth, but whatever it is, you will definitely find happiness in it. But a lot of people are copy cats. Because their friends or coworkers went back to school to get an MBA, they want to do the same irrespective of their dreams or initially defined goals. I am not saying aspirations are bad, what I am saying is that you must listen to your inner voice and follow its counsel; it can never go wrong, stick to what it says and do what it told you to do.

Examine your life and find what makes you happiest, what makes the most meaning to you that even material wealth can't equate, that is your life purpose, focus on that and pursue it with all earnestness, that is the reason why you are here. The failures you see around you are people who can't focus on definite goals. If you pick up one idea and stick with it, it's just a matter of time, you will be so good at it, and in a short while you will be the "go to" person in your field.

For every man there is a plan and purpose, never envy another, because you may not fit into his shoes if that is not the divine plan for you. You are who you are because you were cut fit for your task; you were designed to succeed in the field that has been divinely chosen for you. For every man there is a time appointed, that you exist at this point in time, in history, means you are relevant to your generation; you have something to offer in this here and now. So stop and listen to your heart, what is it that you have that the world is yet to see. Put every distraction aside and search your heart; when you find it, success is inevitable.

The richest men in this world do not come from one particular vocation; neither is one particular vocation an ultimate catapult to riches and happiness. Be a doctor, a lawyer, a mechanic, a house painter, it does not matter, the only thing that matters is to be very happy at what you do and be good at it. I have seen very rich engineers and I have met poor ones. I have seen very wealthy artists and I have met with paupers. I have seen billionaire musicians; also there are lots of poor ones. Are you cut out for the task you are doing right now? Many strive for things that do not belong to them, but as the law is, so will it be, whatsoever you desire you will receive, the only question is, was it divinely planned for you?

Whatever point you are at this time is an indication of how far you have come, and the good things you now enjoy are the benefits accrued to you. Be grateful and appreciate how far you have come, rest assured that the infinite also serves those who wait. In life some people travel light; others are saddled with great responsibilities. Whatever side of the divide you belong, never be disgruntled, because there is a plan and a purpose for everything. Be happy with where you are, love your situation unconditionally! Be cheerful at your tasks and surely you will attract greater opportunities.

The things you seek are also seeking you. So be anxious for nothing, put your mind at rest, and remain focused on your goals, it's just a matter of time, what you seek will be yours. Love unconditionally, no matter how bad the situation, never be fazed by the things you see or feel. In a short time the clouds will clear and the sun will appear in all its glorious brightness. It is the law; you will get exactly what you give – give unconditional love if you want positive changes in your life.

WHAT YOU GIVE, YOU RECEIVE

*R*ecently, I have been having some mind-boggling experiences. But on second thought, these experiences are not new, they have always been there; it's just that I haven't been paying attention until now. I do, naturally, have an inquisitive mind, but as I get older, I am becoming more aware of my surroundings and my daily life experiences. I have noticed a direct correlation between my interactions with fellow human beings and the consequences of such interactions. Based on these observations, I have been able to deduce the hows and whys of many events in my life experiences. A lot of people will dismiss as superstition what I am going to discuss in this chapter, but this book is a chronicle of an old man's empirical evidence of reality, and how these realities correlate with daily life experiences. The complex nature of the human mind, if harnessed to a fine degree, can achieve great phenomena. The human being is supernatural, and if we could only understand this super nature, life would be a lot easier. There is more to the human species than we perceive with our senses, and our life experiences are a reflection of our supernatural nature.

There are lots of definitions of the word "karma." Generally, people refer to karma as fate, but fate is very far from what karma really means. Karma has nothing to do with fate, karma means action, not an effect or result of an action; karma is energy derived from our intentional thoughts and actions, and these thoughts and actions affect our future. What you do now sets the tone for the future, thus, you can change the tone of the future by changing your current action. I am explaining the meaning of karma so you can have a better understanding of what I am going to discuss in this chapter. In this chapter I discuss the effects of our actions, that is, our actions toward one another. The effects of our actions are important because what you give or do to others, you will receive in return.

As a young man, I was pretty careless about life, I was selfish and brutal. I never considered other people's feelings; my desires came first, before those of everyone else. It was a choice of path that left many people devastated, and I was completely oblivious of the consequences of my actions. But now in my old age I see the reflections of my younger years in my current life experiences. One particular event was so vivid it got my attention immediately. In this incident I saw my life play out before me like déjà vu in reverse. I became the brunt of another person's obsessive demand and that woke me up from my selfish slumber. This instance started with a young woman who was particularly nice to me. She gave me some money at a time in my life that I was in need and showed much concern for me. A few weeks later she brought some business to me, which I executed, and she paid me but left a very small fraction of the balance unpaid. I don't know what came over me but I harassed her until I received the last dime, forgetting that this was the same person who gave me a gift of a large sum of money not too long ago. Ten years later, I met a young man who did some work for me; I wanted to encourage him to develop his talent so I brought more business his way and never haggled when he charged a fee. It so happened that I wanted to have him send a document I had already paid for in a different file format, this man insisted I pay the full cost of production that I had already paid. I was in shock because I know he knew I had been very generous with my payments. This incident gave me a jolt because it was a reprisal of my own action against the woman described above. This is just one small instance out of many instances; there are other situations that are very vivid. I would have loved to put some of these experiences down in print, but because those involved would easily recognise them, I'll let them pass. But suffice to say that my life portrayed the fact that the problems we face in life arise from how we serve others.

In life, whatever we do to others we receive in return. I have outstanding empirical evidence that supports this belief. Some skeptics will dismiss such evidence as coincidences. But whether they accept my proposition or not, it will not change the fact of the matter – what you serve others, you will be served in return.

Recently, there has been a big clamour for the law of attraction; people love the law of attraction because it has to do with personal gains. That we can have what we want if we put our attention to getting it is a very exciting proposition, but there is more to life than what we see or perceive. While we can attract everything irrespective of whether other people are getting hurt in the process, we will be accountable for our actions, and this accountability is not in the hereafter (there is no hereafter, anyway), it happens in the here and now. We receive what we serve others in our lifetime. I know this is not a pleasant idea and probably contrary to your theology, but you've got to step back and examine your life and see if what I am saying has any truth in it.

Many religions encompass this truth, but whether by omission or commission they have created loop holes of escape for their members through false doctrines. Some religions introduce sacrifices to wipe away errors. They teach that when you make penance, your errors are wiped out. But when the error doesn't go away, how do you explain that? What do you do? "Oh, you make more sacrifices," their proponents would say. But there is no escape. No amount of sacrifice can avert the consequences of our actions; we are ever in the presence of the consequences of our actions. "What you give, you will receive in return." We will forever bear the brunt of the excesses we enact with one another, and memories of these interactions will be indelibly seared in our memories for the rest of our lives. Like an injury, the pain may be gone but the scar will always remain. You may argue with me till your hair falls out, but you know as well as I do that this is true and the proof is evident in your life. This is our reality. Although there are various forms of denial and labelling that discredit this principle, our lives are a testimony to this law.

There is a reason why this principle holds true; that reason is ONENESS. All humanity is one consciousness; everyone is a varied expression of the same single entity, God, Infinite Spirit, Jah, Allah, whatever name you call it. We all are connected by the web of this one consciousness. The "Egg "is a brief story on the Internet by Andy Weir that explains the nature of who we really are in terms of our oneness with the Infinite. Though I am not sure about the reincarnation part, the essence of our personality as an expression of the Divine is not far from the truth. We are a reflection of one another as much as we are one with the Infinite. My writings are based on my daily life experience, therefore, I can only say what I have experienced. I do not know about reincarnation, and have no reason to believe in it. But in this here and now, we, and I mean all humans, are all connected irrespective of ethnicity, colour, or language. All humanity is one; we are from one source, one life, and one consciousness. When one of us is hurting, we are all hurting. When you wrong another, you have wronged a version of yourself. And with time we experience the consequences of our actions.

There is an ancient saying that nothing happens without an on-looker. We are ever before the watchful presence that is in us, and as us, a presence that pervades the universe, that is in all things. There is no escaping this observing presence; our lives are not hidden from it. Panpsychism tells us that there is consciousness everywhere, but while we cannot at the moment prove that the rock or trees have same consciousness as humans, we know that all humans have one and same consciousness.

I know a man who once dated a girl. He loved this woman but at the same time was careless about their relationship. He cheated on countless occasions, yet she remained faithful. With the flimsiest excuse he broke up with her and married another girl. Fifteen years down the line in the relationship with his new bride, she suddenly turned into his worst nightmare. She became everything he ever dreaded in a woman. He tried his best to salvage his marriage, he became kind in the midst of her hostility, he showed love in spite of her open hatred, he did everything to please her so they could have peace, but all to no avail. He became fed up and decided to walk away, but just at that moment of decision, memories of his previous relationship flashed before his eyes. He remembered how he was cruel to his first love, how she was dedicated to serving and preserving their relationship. She was the perfect wife but he walked away from her, now it was too late because she had moved on.

Problems occurring in our present moment mirror our past errors and we are faced with the measure we meted to others. The man mentioned above would never have realized the pain he had inflicted on his first love, until his wife served him what he served another. Florence Scovel Shinn says that "Life is a mirror, and we find only ourselves reflected in our associates." All our hidden traits, characters, and closet secrets are acted out through our associates. We reap exactly what we sow. The ancient law that said "do unto others as you would have them to do unto you" is based on a true understanding of the intention of the Superconscious for our existence. We are here to love one another, to respect one another, and to care for one another. There is no escaping this divine plan. When we experience consequences of our actions in our daily life activities, the intention is not to punish us for our errors but to point us in the right direction. The Infinite does not derive any pleasure from seeing us suffer, neither does He initiate such pains; we have these experiences so we can learn from them. With such experience we are better equipped to understand what it takes to love and respect one another, and we are supposed to pass these learnings down to our children so that the ultimate plan of the Infinite to have all humanity evolve into Supernatural beings is fulfilled. Paul, in his letter to the Roman believers affirmed this concept when he wrote "For the earnest expectation of the creature waiteth for the manifestation of the sons of God"[1] All humanity is waiting at this threshold of evolution that we might evolve, unfold into oneness with the Infinite in this plane of existence, in other words, to bring the Kingdom of Heaven to Earth.

This concept is in the human psyche but it has been misinterpreted by science. Instead of developing our spirituality, humans have chosen to evolve mentally. The human body was meant to be subject to the inner man, but humans are overwhelmed by the cravings of the physical body and are constantly encouraged to do so through advertising and aggressive marketing strategies. Everything is done as a direct opposite of the Divine plan, thus counterfeiting the original agenda.

The scripture talks about the law of grace. Paul wrote "for ye are saved by grace not of thyself but it is the gift of God"[2] Grace is unmerited favour; it is a situation that occurs outside natural laws; it is an exception to the principle of cause and effect.

Grace is difficult to explain because the reasons behind the "why" are baffling. We can only imagine it is divine intervention. But Grace does not apply when you deliberately take advantage of another person. I heard, and also believed, that once you commit yourself to God all your past errors are forgiven and wiped out. But hey, we are still here on Earth and no one knows your life better than you do, tell me, why are you still suffering the consequences of your past actions despite your new beliefs? It is the pain that got healed, not the scars, scars don't go away, they will forever be a reminder of your errors. There is a just recompense for every action, every deed, and every good or evil we do to another.

We see big business owners oppressing the poor, manipulating countries, and ruining lives. The general consensus is that these super-rich individuals are untouchable. But take a close look at their private lives and see how dark and miserable they are. Their families are in total disarray, hopeless crackheads and sick minds, many have incurable diseases. The business mogul may have successfully wrenched that piece of land from the poor owner but the mogul's children are useless drug addicts. With time all his illicitly acquired fortunes will become desolate, a reward for his greed and oppression.

All persons who choose to torture, punish, steal, or take advantage of another just because they can, shall have their rewards here on Earth, this is not wishful thinking but an empirical law that is unchanging. I have seen it, I have experienced it, and I know it is infallible.

I don't know about heaven or hell, but I do know that there is a reward right here on Earth for those who do not respect the lives of fellow humans in this journey called "life." They may look glamourous on the outside but their lives are a living hell, happiness is but a fleeting experience for them, they keep chasing but never catching.

After many years of careful study of this principle, I developed a personal rule of thumb which says "Because I can, does not mean I should." Do not take advantage of another person just because you can; be considerate and always remember that the measure you mete to others will be meted to you. The principle of cause and effect is not a pleasant topic because people want to exploit one another to their own advantage; in fact, it is the business module of the Western world, but a few who have seen the consequences of this approach do business differently. This is a bitter truth that people don't want to talk about. They would rather eulogise the law of attraction than talk about this principle and its corroboration with what Ms. Lauryn Hill wrote in her song titled "Adam Lives in Theory" – that "fantasy is what people want but reality is what they need." The principle of cause and effect is the reality we all need; it is the truth we all must hear, know, and understand.

I was never given to this way of thinking, as I was raised a Christian. But empirical observation of my life showed proof that every action I engage in with my fellow humans had a consequence. My adherence to this principle has made my life harmonious, and I know it's going to be the same for everyone who strives to maintain peace with one another. And come to think of it, isn't this the reason why we are here on Earth? We are all brothers and sisters sent here to tend to this one giant garden called Earth. Why are we fighting one another, cheating and killing one another? Haven't we observed that the more we are not in harmony, the more we find it difficult to live and to enjoy our lives? Why create divisions through religion, race, colour, and class. Who among you would rush a dying patient to a hospital only to turn away when you discover the doctor on duty has a different racial background? Why allow religion or racial bias to divide us? What is wrong with humanity?! Why are people pushing destructive and baseless agendas? What I see in the world makes my heart recoil. I have seen people rejected at job interviews because of their skin colour. This is disgusting and painful and it is a huge loss to humanity to see the very best hands without opportunities to serve because of baseless racial profiling, gender discrimination, and religious sentiments.

It may take a while, but I know one day people will come to realise that all humanity is one; there are no differences between us. Let us stop pointing fingers at one another. Some say it's the big corporations, but the big corporations are administrated by people so it makes no difference. Let us change the world, let us change the way we think, let us show love to one another because we are all one and same consciousness, the human race is one.

LIVING ABOVE FEAR

*I*n 2012, I was in a state of despair, fear, and worry when suddenly, out of the blue, this question popped into my head: "what is the worst that could possibly happen?" I was jolted by the audacity of this intrusive thought, but when I thought about the question, I realized that, even if the worst happened, there was absolutely nothing I could do but deal with it. If you think back, you will recall that some of the issues that once froze you with fear came and went and you survived them all. We often forget our past victories when we are confronted with new problems.

Fear is just a temporary state of emergency declared by the conscious mind. This temporary state of emergency forces the mind to freeze! In other words, our conscious mind hits the panic button when it cannot produce an immediate solution to a pressing problem. To understand how the mind works, we need to understand that there are three states of consciousness: the conscious, the subconscious, and the superconscious, which is the "I" within or the God mind. The conscious mind is your mental state, this mind is analytical, it processes information, and it tells you what to do, how to do it, and when to do it. The conscious mind feeds the subconscious with thoughts and ideas that the subconscious uses in the present or future, like names of people, places, or things, or procedures such as playing the piano or driving a car. As Charles Haanel put it in the *Masterkey System*, "Ease and perfection depend entirely upon the degree in which we cease to depend upon the consciousness." The subconscious mind uses automated reasoning. It functions based on past reasoning, ideas that have been processed and verified by the conscious mind. Our instinctive reflexes and actions are dependent on our subconscious mind.

The superconscious is the God mind. The superconscious is not influenced by the conscious or the subconscious, in fact it overrides the impressions that the conscious mind has left on the subconscious. The superconscious is the realm of great ideas; this is where insurmountable courage dwells. There is always peace and calm in this realm, nothing ever disturbs or upsets the superconscious mind.

By asking yourself the question "what is the worst that could possibly happen?" your mind transcends the situation. Naturally, the mind moves on to other issues when it loses interest in a present condition. The above question helps to put whatever condition that is bothering you out of the conscious mind. For instance, if a family member is at the point of death, every member of the family is frantic, running everywhere to try to save him, but as soon as he is pronounced dead everything stops. All the worries and apprehension cease because there is no life to save anymore. When you take your mind off an issue, it loses momentum. Momentum in thought is the engine that drives life experience. Remember what I said earlier, a thought persistently held in the mind creates a real life experience. It's the repetitiveness that causes the momentum which in turn creates the life experience. So, the whole idea is to take your mind off the issue so that you become nonresistant to the situation.

The superconscious has your best interests at heart, your life has been preplanned for only good to happen. Whatever circumstance, even if it is negative or catastrophic, the end result will always be for your good. If you can grasp this concept, a lot of situations in your life will become easier to understand. Very few people have any idea about the omnipotent powers of the superconscious that dwells within them. Many clichés about life have been ingrained into our thinking and we have come to believe them to be true, when in fact they are the opposite of what life should be! For instance, we hear "there is suffering before pleasure," "life is a struggle," "it's the survival of the fittest," all these sayings undermine even the lowliest powers of the mind! Everybody knows that owners of businesses are not the ones who do the menial jobs. The hard work is left for the guys who use the least of their mental powers. In the hierarchy of power, those who use the least of their mental powers are at the very bottom; these are the muscle men, the cleaners, the errand boy or girl who does the menial jobs. On the next higher level are those who have mastered the use of their subconscious minds, these are the business magnates, the skilled trades, great composers of symphonies and professionals in various fields. Finally, at the very top level of mind powers are the mental masters who have been able to establish a connection with the "I" within. These people have command over their bodies as well as their minds and can channel their powers into various forms. If they choose to affect others, they can. They are considered mystics because they operate in a higher realm. They can induce healing; they are telepathic, clairvoyant, and have high extrasensory perception. This is the realm in which Jesus and many other mystics operated. So you see that the ordinary man who is suffering is suffering because he is ignorant of the forces within him. In letting limitations determine your fate, you yield to your lesser power. Within this realm of lesser power dwell all base thoughts such as fear, jealousy, greed, anger, frustration, and self-limiting beliefs.

Among the above mentioned vices, fear is the worst; fear is like having someone take over your home and wreak havoc. This state is what Apostle Paul referred to as being carnally minded[1] – a state in which the self does not acknowledge the supernatural abilities within, does not acknowledge the presence of the superconscious or the God within. In chapter 8: 8 of that same scripture, Paul says the carnal mind is enmity with God. You must understand these ancient teachings so that you can make good use of the information provided. God dwells within you and you dwell in God; in other words, you and God are the same, which is why the scripture confirmed that "ye are Gods!"[2] When the scripture says that the carnal mind is enmity with God, it is saying that the carnal mind or base thinking or having a lesser view of the potential of the superconscious within you is your enemy, for you and God are the same! You are much higher than you think, you are limitless, you can be, do, or have anything. Living in fear is living way below your potential. Fear has no power over the evolved mind. You can recreate your world if you master your fears.

When we forget the great battles we have won, very small issues send us scuttling for cover. We must realize that no matter what happens in our lives, everything will eventually right itself. Be calm and stay put, knowing that there is always good in the midst of every bad situation, no matter how bad the condition may be. Just like the oyster that creates a beautiful gem out of an irritation, your current challenge might be your pivot for your next level in life. This is not some philosophical statement, but a fact that I have experienced time and again. When the writers of the scriptures said "be anxious for nothing"[3] they spoke from a resounding understanding that good will always come, just as day follows night.

FIND YOUR HAPPY PLACE

*E*veryone who wants to see positive changes in his life must first seek the peace within or the divine self, in other words he has to come to unity with the divine self or the "I" that is within. The "I" within is the same as the universal "I", the difference is only in degree. The "I" within has the same character and ability to do that which the universal "I" does. The degree to which we manifest the powers of the universal "I" or the superconscious is based on our consciousness of this power, for power is based on consciousness of power. You can manifest only what is possible within your known abilities.

When you are at peace with your divine self, this state is reflected in your daily life experiences. Life experiences are reflections of thoughts, words, and actions. Nothing happens by chance. This principle is not new; it is emphasized in most religions. For instance, the scriptures say "keep thy heart with all diligence, for out of it are the issues of life,[1]" meaning that out of it come life experiences, thoughts create life experiences!

The way to a joyous peaceful life starts with keeping a close tab on your thoughts. Learn to remain unfazed by circumstances. Learn to remain contented and undisturbed by events, be in a state of equilibrium, and do not be excited or anxious about any situation. This un-swayed positioning is where the "I" within dwells, this is where you meet with divinity half way. The "I" within, who is one with the great "I am" or the super-consciousness or God, does not know or recognize or associate with negative conditions. It sees only possibilities in every circumstance. To illustrate this I'll give you an instance. A terrible incident occurs and a man falls into deep sorrow. He has two options. Either he remains where he is, wallowing in his sorrow, or he decides to forget the past and move on. The moment he says "it's enough" and rouses himself to get back on his feet he becomes energized, a new man emerges. How did he overcome the emotions that were spiraling downward? We must realize that in spite of every existing tragedy there also exists a force of positive change waiting to obey man's command the moment he reaches out to it. When you tap into the strength of the "I," the strength you need materializes. Giving up adds no value to your circumstance, but maintaining a joyous positive posture changes everything for the better.

Being in your happy moment or aligning yourself with the "I" within is all the magic you need to open the door to true happiness. Don't allow events and things you see around you define how you feel or stall the arrival of all that you seek or want. For as long as you live and as long as you want to maintain that joyous, peaceful state of mind, you must strive to remain aligned with the "I" within, even when you find yourself in situations that provoke a negative reaction. Remember that in yielding to your outward challenges you displace your alignment with the infinite. In moments of separation you get short circuited, and everything stops.

Have you noticed that you are the most creative when you are the happiest? The reason is because you activated your connection with your divine self, and your divine self-resides in a happy place. Whenever you maintain your happy stance, divinity is already there, awaiting your arrival! In linking with your joyful self you are automatically linked with the source energy whose origin you are. The "I" within you is ever joyful and in this state you are at your creative best. It is in the place of alignment that your strength, your skills, your creative abilities lie.

The universal "I" expresses itself through you! Therefore you must strive to maintain your inner peace so that there is a continuous flow. And just like apostle Paul said, "I keep under my body, and bring it into subjection"[2]. It has to be a conscious, continuous process of monitoring your emotions, and actions, making sure that you choose joy over despair, you choose hope over defeat, you choose happiness over sadness and anger, and you choose nonresistance over negative conditions. You might find yourself in painful situations, but when you refuse to be disturbed by any situation, it fades out from your life completely. In fact, such situations exist because you are paying attention to them. But maintaining a good attitude in spite of a negative condition makes a bad situation tolerable. And from being tolerable it gravitates to being pleasant. The pleasantness comes from the fact that you now see things that were not visible to you before due to the blindness caused by your negativity. After a while the negative situation fades away naturally.

The scripture says "seek ye first the kingdom of God and its righteousness and all other things shall be added unto you."[3] The kingdom is that inner place of the "I" within, that point where your connection with the infinite is at its best.

You must have noticed that when you are in an emotional state nothing seems to work. Calm yourself by seeking alignment with the "I" within. The Jewish prophet Isaiah said, "In returning and rest shall you be saved, in quietness and confidence shall be your strength."[4] Your realignment with source energy, God, is your redemption; this is the kingdom that Christ taught that we should seek. And he said the kingdom is within you![5] Therefore realign yourself with the "I" within and everything you seek will fall into place.

Everyday strive to remain in your happy place, create moments and memories that will trigger this divine fusion. The benefits of aligning with the infinite are immeasurable, and above all you will experience your very best self when you are fully connected with the "I" within.

Life can deliver a full package of disastrous surprises, and the choices you make will either make or break you. Self-pity, anger, and blaming others will keep you in a place of resistance, whereas your freedom arrives when you laugh at life and let go. No matter what you see, feel, or think, never be disturbed by circumstances, because you can change circumstances by changing the way you think and feel about them. Whatever challenge stands in your way, bless it and let it go, never allow anything to stand between you and your alignment with your divine self. Entertaining negative thoughts will deprive you of your joy, and assign disappointment to every effort you make. But in letting go, and focusing on pleasant thoughts, the human becomes Divine, the natural becomes Supernatural. In that place of divine fusion the new you is born.

Things may go terribly wrong in your relationships, and you have the urge to fix them. If your initial move for peace is denied, don't let it bother you, for that will put you in a place of resistance. Be at peace with yourself and with the situation, it will gradually fade away. If persons antagonize you, do not hold a grudge; rather, bless them and let the matter be, because if you persist in getting to the bottom of these issues, I assure you, there'll be no end, for some people are more equipped for trouble than others. In the words of Rae Zander in her online radio show, *Everyday Attraction* said "When people are so attached to their story they can't hear you", in fact the more words you speak the less they'll hear. So, when you find yourself in an unpleasant situation, bless it and let it go. It may seem like you have been shortchanged, it may seem that justice has been denied, but greater battles have been won in silence and quietness. As all humanity is one, whatever you do to another you do to yourself. Life is a constant reflection of what we serve others, irrespective of religion or position in the spiritual hierarchy.

In life there will always be situations where you will be offended or you will offend others. Your ability to resolve these issues without creating disharmony within yourself is your only hope of salvation. Do not be the one who carries the big stick of justice, irrespective of how right you think you are. The universe has its own ways of paying back. For every cause, there is an effect and for every action there is a consequence.

It is better to be the offended than to be the offender because it is much easier to neutralize disharmony within yourself than to appease another, hoping he forgives. Your ultimate goal is to avoid being displaced from your alignment with the infinite. Let go of anger and frustration, forgive everyone who wronged you, it's all for your own good. What you lose as a result of a difficult situation can never be compared with what is in store for you in the future. I know from my experience that challenges are prerequisites for growth. There are lessons to be learned from every experience and I assure you that these challenges are preparatory grounds for future expansion. People who put you through painful experiences are not your enemies; in fact you should be thanking them and blessing them for being instrumental to your growth.

In forgiving and letting go, your spirit is free to roam the universe and connect with the forces of creation. Your creative juices start to flow again; the best of you is suddenly released. Being a creative person myself, I know that the best ideas lie in a mind that is free from every negative condition. A free mind is the temple of creativity; un-forgiveness, anger and negativity clutter the mind and stall creativity.

Never focus on how bad a situation is or has been, or how

badly you have been hurt. Forget about what he said or she said or did, you will only make yourself more miserable if you persist in this line of thinking. Nobody is responsible for your happiness, you are responsible for you. You don't need others to be happy before you can be happy, others don't have to feel good before you feel good. You must feel good irrespective of how every other person feels or what he or she thinks because only you can determine how you want to feel. You are not here to live your life through someone else's window because you are the door to your own joy; therefore your happiness depends on you. Seek the joy within and remain in your happy place.

Always think of reasons why you should be happy, seek happy things and happy thoughts. Surround yourself with happy conditions. Focus your mind on things that are pleasant, remain boisterous and joyous, find that happy place and remain there, see every moment as a blast, an opportunity to be the best that you can be. Even when all seems to be in chaos, remain calm. The divine self is always in a joyous and happy mood, get connected.

When you woke up this morning, you were happy until you remembered the things that went wrong yesterday. Why would you dwell on the sorrows of yesterday when the abundance of today is yet to be unraveled? Forget yesterday and live in the moment. This moment, this very second, is a brand new time, a brand new place in reality. Don't let life's circumstances push you into reactionary living, be deliberate and decisive in your actions, and laugh at life when things are not working out. In a short time whatever situation that is bothering you will be over.

DIVINE FUSION

*M*an's spirituality has often been associated with religion; but because religion has been plagued by charlatans, many people have been thrown off the path of truth, having drawn the conclusion that man's spiritual nature does not exist.

However there is a higher consciousness that dwells within man, some call it God or Buddha or the Superconscious or the Christ within. Irrespective of the name called, this consciousness is the super self. This consciousness knows no limitations and can never be restricted by any condition. Although anyone can activate this connection whenever needed, very few people consciously tap into this force.

All humanity is one; the consciousness of one man is the same as the consciousness of every man. When we manifest this consciousness in our lives it is reflected in the things we do, our careers, our goals and our dreams. When we reinforce a positive attitude, we are acting on the influence of the superconscious.

If the consciousness revealed in each and every one of us is the same consciousness that created the universe, then the scripture must be right when it says "Ye are gods"[1] because we are all parts of the big whole. The level of consciousness we have in our lives determines to what extent we make these manifestations, and if we choose to obliterate this consciousness, it stays quiet until we reactivate it. It's like a hurricane lamp, we may choose to dim the light but that does not take away its luminous capacity, and if we choose to turn it on full blast, everyone will enjoy the bright light.

The infinite, God, is the source of all things big and small; we are limitless in our potentials if we activate our connections with the infinite. If we agree that the power that created the universe is the same consciousness that is focused on everyone, nothing can stand in the way of our capacities to achieve any goal or dream. The big question is how do we consciously cultivate and activate this power that is within so that we can maximize its awesome potential?

When we study the pagan or the Pentecostal worshippers, at some point in their worship, they come to a place of reverence and rest. They acknowledge the presence of the infinite at this point, yet it is not rest really, for within this rest, there are vibrations and the vibrations are at their peak which makes them seem to be at rest. Vibration is one of the seven hermetic principles in the *Kybalion*, written under the pseudonym of "the Three Initiates." It is said that a vibration can be so high in frequency that it may seem to be at rest, like the spokes of a bicycle wheel blur when the wheel spins at very high speed. I'll call this point of rest, this point of high frequency vibration, "divine fusion." Divine fusion brings man to a place of rest yet not rest, a place of yieldedness and total submission to the infinite, a point of nonresistance. This is the point where man and divinity fuse to become one, a point where the self is lost and the "I" within merges with the great "I am", a harmonious seamless connection. Divine fusion is beyond regular religious worship, it brings man up to the level of the infinite. The old concept of worship postulates that man must revere the

Supreme Being. Often this Supreme Being must be appeased through sacrifices or other forms of worship, else something would go wrong with the believer's life. This concept suits those who created it, for man wants control over his fellow man. This idea places God high above and beyond man's reach, which is the exact opposite of what God or the infinite spirit really is. God dwells in man! Christ tried to explain this in the scriptures but the Pharisees were offended because they said he equated himself to God - John 10:30-39.

In divine fusion, man identifies with divinity and the oneness that exists between the creator and the created. It is a process of seeking connection, a connection that already exists but is constantly truncated by emotions. It is an expression of self as well as a release of self. It's like fine tuning a radio station to get its clearest signal. When locked in, there is a smooth flow that results in relaxation, absolute quietness, sometimes leading to joyful tears or laughter. There is a release and a receiving of energies. Divine fusion is letting go, a surrendering to this higher power, this is the point where you ask and it is given, what you seek, you find.

Thus divine fusion is an essential tool in the creation and manifestation of desires, because you are right there, where the creative process is taking place – Man meets God. There is no resistance at this point, only the seamless transmission of energies; this is man's place of rest. Prophet Isaiah put it nicely in chapter 30:15 "In returning and rest shall ye be saved, in quietness and in confidence shall be your strength"

I have never practiced yoga, but I have experienced divine fusion time and again, and each time I am in divine fusion, I get transformed and energized. There are days I get the urge to get connected. Those moments always turn out beautiful. They say men are not supposed to cry, but these are the moments of shameless releases of tears, you can feel this life force coming through, you can feel the love, the warmth and the joy within.

And at the end, there is a calmness that is beyond expression, a quietness that is so sweet and warm. I don't know what works for you, but whatever you do, as long as it brings you to that point of union with divinity, that's all you need to do to make those manifestations become real.

HOW TO CREATE DIVINE FUSION

As far as I know, there are no specific formulas or incantations or methods to get into Divine fusion. Personally, I find it easier getting into the flow very early in the morning but that does not mean evenings are not good. In fact, there are days when I get back from my job feeling really exhausted and I just want to utter a quick gratitude prayer for a successful day and boom! He takes over completely, bringing me down to a solid moment of divine experience. However in the mornings, the body and mind have rested, there are no momentums of some unresolved arguments or tasks waiting to be completed. The serenity of the early morning channels this fusion easily.

You may start with a prayer of gratitude, concentrating on all the good things you have experienced in your life. Relax and let go of thoughts and worries – appreciate every gift you have received, the love you experience today, the joy of being alive, the provisions and supplies for all your daily needs, love from family and friends, favour, opportunities, the list can be endless when you break it down to these simple things. Another way of getting into divine fusion is through singing or listening to inspirational music. You can easily get spirited away when you are in the mood of a song. Choose the kind of music that works for you.

You may have these moments as a group (like a family) if it's well coordinated and the moment is reverenced. A group divine fusion brings about a special bond among the family members; however, the individual moments must be practiced before or after the group sessions because it helps develop personal relationship with the infinite. You must have that special time, alone with the infinite, because often the infinite is full of pleasant surprises.

In conclusion, divine fusion brings you to the point of unity with the infinite, thus easing out all your stresses and worries, bringing peace, joy, and rest and making manifest all you seek or want. There are no designated places for divine fusion, for he whom you seek is within you. You carry him around and about all day long, that is why Paul asked, "know you not that your body is the temple of the Holy Ghost?"[2] Remember also that Christ said in John 4:21: "believe me, the hour cometh, when ye shall neither in this mountain, nor yet at Jerusalem, worship the Father."[3] Why? Because you are the temple! You carry the holy of holies with you; you are the dwelling place of the most high. You don't need any intermediary or some high priest to be your intercessor; those are relics of defective beliefs. He who made you also equipped you with a communication device which is your higher self or the "I" within. He left a residue of himself within you so you can keep in touch whenever and wherever you want. You are more than just flesh and blood, you came from the divine mind, therefore you operate above the limitations of your physical self, and nothing, absolutely nothing, can stand in your way. Day after day you must seek to be in union with the infinite; therein lies your power, your health, and all you ever wanted in life. There is nothing you cannot do, be, or have because you are superhuman, and the only way to remain in this state of super-human-ness is through divine fusion.

FAITH AND GRACE

There are certain phenomena for which there is no physical proof. For example, there is no empirical evidence that a faith in God or any other deity has a direct correlation with human activities. But can we say that because something is not provable it is unreal? Atoms cannot be seen, do we say atoms don't exist?

The preceding chapters of this book have dealt with the conscious mind, the subconscious mind, and the superconscious, or the God-within. I have also mentioned the use of affirmations or meditations, and being in the silence to initiate communication with the Divine. But having faith in God, and the exercise of that faith, bring us to a different level of discussion. I reserved this topic for a later section of this book because of its religious connotation. We naturally exercise faith at every moment of our existence, and when we do, we do not attribute religion to such decisions. In other words, faith is a way of life for all humanity.

The fact that you got out of bed, the fact that you went to work, the fact that you boarded an aeroplane to fly from one destination to another, are all acts of faith or a belief that the future will always resemble the past; today will be like yesterday, the sun will rise in the morning, there will always be enough air for everyone to breath, day will always follow night.

But what if there are clear instances of uncertainty in an action you intend to take? What gives you confidence that your action will have the same results as other times? Why do we experience fear when we take certain actions or face situations where conditions are not met to guarantee our safety? Hypothetically, if you were told just before you boarded an aeroplane that the designated pilot called in sick, but because they want to meet the regular schedule, the airport janitorial assistant has volunteered to take his place. Would you want to fly on that day, even if it's very important that you get to your destination? We use our intellect and our physical senses to decide whether situations impose certain dangers.

However, our senses can give us a false perception of security, because dangers we don't know about don't bother us. People regularly board airplanes, assuming that the airplanes are safe and the pilots are competent. But how can you tell if a pilot is competent? I have yet to see a passenger demand proof of a pilot's qualifications before boarding a plane. Everyone boards a plane confidently at the airline of their choice and assumes they will get home safely. This is what I mean when I say that we exercise faith every day and this has nothing to do with our religious beliefs. Faith is a way of life for humans, we believe, we trust, we hope that everything will be the same as usual.

Some time ago, I visited Charlottetown on Prince Edward Island (PEI). My flight back from PEI was uneventful, but just as we were about to touch down in Montreal, the air hostess, who was very funny and lively, thanked everyone for boarding this airline and said, "and by the way, please give it up for xxx, this is his very first flight on a commercial airline! Everybody cheered but I was stunned. I thought, if the airline had announced earlier that the pilot for the day was an apprentice, I bet no one would have boarded that flight. But this is how the ordinary person's faith works, what you don't know you assume is okay. However, this type of faith is quite different from the kind of faith I am going to discuss in this chapter.

Courage is being aware of the danger in performing an act but doing it anyway. Faith is a belief in something that cannot be measured or proven scientifically. Faith is more than hope. Hope is an optimistic feeling, whereas faith is a feeling that something is certain. Many successes in life are built on faith; faith is the engine that drives many innovations and new inventions. Can faith help you get a job? Can it help you win a legal case? Can it help you heal physically?

Our bodies interpret our physical experiences, but in order to rein our body into harmony with the superconscious or God, we need to activate our faith. Through faith in the divine we bring the superconscious into conscious experience. It is the activation of our faith that brings us in alignment with the Infinite Spirit, thus God is manifest in our lives. We are aligned with God through faith, this kindles the knowledge and confidence that He lives and dwells in us.

Over the course of writing this book I have provided instances in which the powers of the mind can be used to achieve goals, dreams, and desires. But what I have hitherto failed to mention was that all these instances are subject to God's Grace. Such Grace is often over-looked by people who profess to use the powers of the mind. But I have been a practitioner of mind action for over a decade and I know that mind actions can fail, not because the mind is powerless against the surrounding conditions, but because there is One who is greater that I, One who is in control and sees the future from the past and knows better what choices would suit me. So, while it is a good thing to use the powers of the mind, we must yield our desires to the will of the Father and let it happen by His grace. My favourite teacher, Florence Scovel Shinn, consistently emphasised that when we write an affirmation for a desire or a goal, it should always end with "by the Grace of God in perfect ways." No matter how powerful you may consider your psychic powers, it's all subject to the Grace of the Infinite. After many years of experiencing disappointments in attempting to do things through sheer willpower, I was humbled and submitted to God's Grace. I came to realize that it is not my will, but His will that allows me to achieve my goals. I exist not to fulfil my bodily pleasures but to live for the One who dwells within me.

As a physical being, I have a lot of inadequacies. I am a man of average height, I do not have physical combat abilities, neither do I have a very high IQ to balance my lack of physical strength. I am not street smart, therefore, I am prone to getting whipped by criminally minded persons. But like the proverbial Nigerian saying: "God swats flies for cows without tails," I have found security and defence in trusting God's Grace. I have been through countless hopeless situations, and how I got out of them still amazes me, but certainly it is not by the effort of *my* will. This might sound surprising to people who assume that a man who talks about the power of the mind should be living a charmed life, but this is far from my experience. I do have supernatural occurrences, but they are subject to the Father's plan, and they occur only when I align my desires with the Infinite and allow His Grace to supersede. Any great mystic knows that it is not he that does the work but the Father who dwells within.[1]

Twelve years ago, when I first came across the New Thought teachings that developed in the United States in the 19th century, possibly based on the unpublished writings of Phineas Quimby, I was as arrogant as I was obsessed. I stood my ground on all my mental demands, and my brutish faith seem to work for a while until I came to a crossroads where all my arrogant moves failed and I sobered up. In fact, early chapters of this book still have some cocky elements, as they were written at the early stages of my current beliefs. However, as my eyes opened to deeper truths, I realized that it is the Father who does the work.

We are One with the Infinite for He dwells in us and as us, but He is not us in totality. We must understand Him as well as His overall function in the universe, and acknowledge His presence and revere Him. Knowing the Infinite puts you in a relationship with Him and to know that He is the overseer of all your affairs. He is the wind beneath your wings and the force that generates your existence, so that even if you think you can do all things, you need to understand that your power comes through His indwelling presence. Make no mistakes about what I am saying, God dwell in us, we are conduits for His expression, just as a glass of water fetched from the ocean is not the totality of all the water in the sea, but that which is in the glass is just a small part of the water in the ocean, so are we as Gods, our human lives are only but a tiny expression of the God Head. Jolted into a realization of my physical limitations and my intellectual inadequacies, I have learned to depend on God's Grace for help with my problems.

An incident comes to mind. A series of financial misfortunes prompted me to put my house up for sale, as I was convinced that it was the best option to resolve my financial crisis. But as soon as I accepted a buyer's offer, I discovered an error that arose from some miscalculations at the bank that would make the sale of the property a huge financial risk. I didn't want to sell any more! I quickly told my realtor that I want to pull out of the deal. But she said it was too late as the offer was already pending. I broke out in a cold sweat, what was I going to do? Because all my savings went into financing the initial purchase, the sale would completely destroy my life. Many nights I just sat and stared into the dark, completely lost in thought. I couldn't sleep, think, or work. I lost my appetite for food, I was at the edge of a nervous breakdown. But just in the nick of time I remembered one of my own teachings. (It's amazing how easily you forget the things you know when you let stress confuse your mind).

Recall that I discussed "guided positive speak" (GPS) in chapter 19. GPS is muttering positive words under your breath throughout your waking moments to address a pressing challenge. From my experience, classic affirmations do not work in a mind wrenching situation such as mine, because in writing an affirmation you would want to mention the particular situation and the result you want to achieve, and that is where the problem of anxiety lies. Classic affirmations tend to magnify the problem, because one is focused on the problem itself. When you are focused on a problem you tend to imagine how bad it could get, and the more you think about it, the more you feel the magnitude of your trouble. But this is a trick of the mind because at the present moment, that problem does not exist; the present moment is free from any pressure, circumstances, or situation. Using classic affirmations in situations like this is like fighting a multi-headed monster; when you slay one head, another appears somewhere else, and it is a loop of constant battles and fear.

Now, there are times and places where classic affirmations are required. But for mind boggling situations such as mine, it was best to apply GPS. GPS brings you down to the present moment and defuses the tension of the situation. There are no pressures in the present moment, no fears or anxiety, because it contains nothing, no carryovers from previous experiences, and the future is yet to be lived; the present moment is a peaceful moment in time and space. We are commanded by sages to live in the present moment and project that moment into the next moment, and continually live in the present moment, moment after moment. I explained the process of GPS as blending things you see at the present moment into your GPS, thus keeping you grounded in the moment. This grounding obliterates residual fears since they are in the past. So, back to my legal quagmire, I started to speak:

Infinite Spirit, the great omnipotent One, I celebrate this day, this moment, this now moment. It is so much joy to bask in your presence and to enjoy the goodness, the joy, and the love of life. I thank you for this present moment, that I am free, free to be the very best of me, knowing that you are always with me, as me and within me as my guide and help. My life experiences do not define me, these experiences are but foot stools that lead to greater experiences of you. I give thanks that even though my life experiences may differ from my heart's desire, in reality I know everything is working together for my good, therefore my current challenge has no foothold on me because I can perceive the end from the beginning and I know only good will manifest. ... As I mentioned in chapter 19, this talk could happen while driving, or at work, and you blend the things you observe in your present moment with your talk; for instance, if you are going into a meeting you might add ... as I step into this meeting it's going to be a fantastic moment, as we will be making important decisions this day. Everyone will be in harmony with my new ideas and good things will come out of our deliberations. If you are driving, you might add ... The roads are safe, all the drivers on this road are considerate and patient, and I will get to my destination in good time ..., etc.

Now, to bring GPS home to the heart of the issue, first, build up your confidence and faith through your personal experiences with the Infinite. So, I continued ... I recall time past when I was in dire situations, You stood by me and rescued me. This is no different, what I am going through right now will soon pass. You have consistently been my defence and protection, therefore, my confidence is not shaken. I recall 2007 when I was involved in a car accident, but came out without a scratch. You were there when my supervisor threatened to fire me for no reason; You turned the situation around and got me promoted. When I was given 24 hours to quit my rented room, miraculously, You provided an accommodation that far exceeded where I was living. Therefore, this present situation is no different, no one can take what is mine by Divine right. You said, "you will overturn and overturn and overturn until he comes whose turn it is, and you will give it him."[2] Infinite Spirit, this house is mine by Divine right, my ignorance and disobedience has driven me to this point, I should have trusted You and Your promises, knowing that You will never leave nor forsake me,[3] but in Your multitude of mercies, remember me, remember moments that I had made You proud, moments when You identified with me and said "this is my beloved son"; and just like a father would look at his beloved baby child and curdle him in his arms, remember these moments and let your love shine through …

Because of my initial Christian background, I find it easy to pull scripture from the Bible to boost my GPS. But GPS language is not Christian-specific, it works with any monotheist belief. As I have consistently maintained that the Infinite Spirit is One, it makes no difference if you are a Muslim, a Buddhist, or a Rastafarian, there is One Consciousness that pervades the universe, and to that Consciousness we have given different names. So, a Muslim doing GPS could say: "Allah is the best provider,[4] this is the best day of my life, I am excited at every opportunity that comes my way; good people, friends, are coming my way, I expect pleasant surprises as I go through my day …." In my case, I would say: "All my needs are met this day as help comes from unexpected places. Your words tell me You call a bird of prey from the east, a man from a distant land, to execute Your counsel.[5] I am getting help from strangers in strange places, I am particularly favoured this day, as good and great things glide toward me."

You can practice GPS anywhere because you are muttering under your breath, or saying it in your head without moving your lips, which is my favourite way, and nobody will ever know you are practicing GPS. Using GPS is a very powerful experience.

If you sturdy the pattern of the words in my GPS, you'll find that they are not making any particular demand on the situation that is bothering me, but they are reminding the Infinite of our special relationship and at the same time imploring the intervention of His Grace. This is the opposite of what an affirmation does; an affirmation claims a right. To affirm is to reenforce, to make a demand. You will also notice that because these words are not forcefully making a demand, you feel light about your condition. In fact, I forget about my condition as soon as I go deep into GPS. The memories of past victories and my relationship with the Infinite begin to swirl through my consciousness, and the pressure and anxiety dissipate.

GPS is *not* a light exercise. It is a focused exercise that can drain your energy if it is really intense. The intensity heightens when you try to counter the pressure of your anxiety, but at the same time, you will notice that you are not afraid; you don't feel fear, but there is inner propulsion to continually use GPS because it has already generated a momentum that won't dissipate.

We have already discussed the power of words; we said that words are vocalized thoughts. The mind can only hold only one thought at a time; if you choose to use GPS, it becomes the predominant thought and replaces your anxious thoughts. After using GPS for six days with regard to my situation, I got a call from my realtor saying the buyer was no longer interested in my property - I was free!

This is an example of faith in the Infinite and His Grace at work. I cannot lay claim to any magical formula that dictated the final outcome of my situation. But just as you hold petals of flowers in the palm of your hand and you release them to the wind, so also we are expected to let the Infinite take charge over our affairs, being in total submission to His Will, knowing that all things will work for our individual and for our collective good.

REFERENCES

Alexander, Linda Lewis (2007), New Dimensions in Women's Health. Sudbury, Massachusetts : Jones and Bartiett Publishers.

Allen, James (1903), As a Man Thinketh. The Savoy Publishing Company Information retrieved from: www.jamesallenlibrary.com

Amplified Bible (AMP).

Baker, Raymond Charles - Science of Mind Magazine, August 1952.

Barnes, J. (ed) 1985: The complete works of Aristotle. NJ: Princeton university press.

Brown, Lachlan (2017),_ Karma definition: Most people are wrong about the meaning. Retrieved from: https://ideapod.com/heres-great-explanation-karma-really-means-can-improve-life/

Canadian women's health network (2012), "Body image and the media". Retrieved from:www.cwhn.ca/node/40776

Corelli, Marie (1911), The Life Everlasting: A Reality of Romance. London: Methuen. Information retrieved from: www.wiseoldgoat.com

The Dhammapada: The Buddha's path of wisdom (1985) Translated by Acharya Buddharakkhita

Descartes, Rene. (1911), The Philosophical works of Descartes. Cambridge University press. Internet Encyclopedia of Philosophy.1996. Translated by Elizabeth S. Haldane.

Dispenza, Joe (2007). Evolve Your Brain: The Science of Changing Your Mind. Deerfield Beach, Florida: Health communications Inc.

Donna Summer (1989), from the song "Break away" Songwriters : Stock/Aitken/Waterman. Published by Sony/ATV Music Publishing LLC, Universal Music Publishing Group.

Eating Disorders Coalition. "Facts about eating disorders. What the research shows" Retrieved from: http://eatingdisorderscoalition.org.s208556.gridserver.com/couch/uploads/file/fact-sheet_2016.pdf

Ford, Henry. (Quote). Originally printed by the Reader's Digest in September, 1947. Retrieved from Quote Investigator:www.quoteinvestigator.com/2015/02/03/you-can/

Ford, Henry. (Went Bankrupt, Now Worth Millions! by Michael Dunlop. Retrieved from: www.incomediary.com/went-bankrupt-now-worth-millions

Forgiveness (From my childhood book on quote; date and author unknown) the metaphorical framework of this quote has an extensive history: http://quoteinvestigator.com/2013/09/30/violet-forgive

Gates, Bill. (Biography) Retrieved from : https://en.wikipedia.org/wiki/Bill_Gates

Ginsberg, Louis. From the Poem "Love that is Hoarded" Retrieved from www: thedistinctdot.com/tag/louis-ginsberg

Goethe, Johann Wolfgang Von (1982), Bk. II, Ch. 5; source: Die Wahlverwandtschaften, Hamburger Ausgabe, Bd. 6 (Romane und Novellen I), dtv Verlag, München, p. 397 (II.5)

Graves, R. M.A (1811). The Meditations of the Emperor, Marcus Aurelieus Antoninus. London: W.Baynes

Google answer
Google Answers (2003). "Thoughts per day". Retrieved from
:
www.answers.google.com/answers/threadview/id/149262.html
Haanel, F. Charles (1919). The Masterkey System. Saint
Louis, MO: Inland Printery (Info source : www.sacred-texts.com)
Harley Davidson Motorbike. (History) Retrieved from:
https://en.wikipedia.org/wiki/Harley-Davidson
Longfellow, Henry Wadsworth (Poem), Retrieved from:
http://www.quotationspage.com/quote/38988.html
Hicks, Esther and Jerry (2007), The Astonishing Power of
Emotions. Carlsbad, USA: Hay House, Inc
Hill, Lauryn (2002) Adam lives in theory: Sony/ATV Music
Publishing LLC. MTV Unplugged.
Jackson, Michael Joseph. (Biography) Retrieved from:
https://en.wikipedia.org/wiki/Michael_Jackson
Jeremy Adam Smith (2014), Scientific Insights from the
Greater Good Gratitude Summit. Retrieved from:
http://greatergood.berkeley.edu/article/item/new_insight-
s_from_the_gratitude_summit
Jordan, Jeffery Michael. (Biography) Retrieved from :
https://en.wikipedia.org/wiki/Michael_Jordan
King James Bible
Linkedin (2012), Cool Careers: LinkedIn Research Reveals
Data about the Top Childhood Dream Jobs:
http://press.linkedin.com/News-Releases/150/Cool-Careers-
LinkedIn-Research-Reveals-Data-About-the-Top-
Childhood-Dream-Jobs
Merriam-Webster's Collegiate® Dictionary, 10th edition
(1999)
Media Smarts- Canada's Centre for Digital and Media
Literacy "Body image-Photo Manipulation". Retrieved from:
http://mediasmarts.ca/body-image/body-image-photo-manip-

ulation

Napoleon Hill and W. Clement Stone (1960), Success Through Positive Mental Attitude. New York: Pocket Books

National Association of Anorexia Nervosa and Associated Disorders. "Fast Facts - Media's effect on body image": http://depts.washington.edu/thmedia/view.cgi?page=fast-facts&section=bodyimage

New King James Bible

Nietzsche, Friedrich (1888), Twilight of the Idols, or, How to Philosophize with a Hammer (Publisher un-known)

Nightingale, Earl (1958), the Strangest Secrete. Nightgale-Conant audio Publication

MMO Champion (2009), Thread: Why do I hate the sound of my 'real' voice? Retrieved from:
www.mmo-champion.com/threads/1135073-Why-do-I-hate-the-sound-of-my-real-voice

Oatman Jr, Johnson (1897), from the song "Count Your Blessings" Retrieved from www. library. timelesstruths.org/music

Peck, M. Scott M.D. The Road Less Traveled (2003) New York: Touchstone. Section ii (Love) page 94

Quimby, Phineas Parkhurst (1863), Disease ii and Disease iii (1864). Phineas Parkhurst

Quimby's writings: http://www.ppquimby.com/articles/list_chron.htm Copyright ©2002 – 2016 Ronald A. Hughes

Reagan, Ronald Wilson. (Biography) Retrieved from: https://en.wikipedia.org/wiki/Ronald_Reagan

Ritu Ghatourey. (Quote) Retrieved from: www.searchquotes.com/quotation/
The_whole_world_will_tell_you_who_you_are.
_until_you_tell_the_world./462231/

Roget, Peter. (Biography) Retrieved from: https://en.wikipedia.org/wiki/Peter_Mark_Roget

Ruse, Michael (2019), A Meaning to Life, New York, USA: Oxford University Press.

Sanders, Harland David. (Biography) Retrieved from : https://en.wikipedia.org/wiki/Colonel_Sanders

Shinn, Florence Scovel (1925), The Game of Life and How to Play it. New York: Self Published

Shinn, Florence Scovel (1928), Your word is your wand. New York: Self Published

Sony Corporation. (History) Retrieved from: https://www.sony.net/SonyInfo/CorporateInfo/History/SonyHistory/1-01.html

The Three Initiates (1908), Kybalion, Chicago: The Yogi Publication. Society Masonic Temple

Theodore Roosevelt (Quote) retrieved from: http://www.goodreads.com/quotes/tag/comparing

Unity world headquarters at Unity Village. How gratitude changes everything. USA: Unity Village.

1901 NW Blue

Weir, Andy: The egg – http://www.galactanet.com/oneoff/theegg_mod.html

Wood, A. M., et al., Gratitude and well-being: A review and theoretical integration,Clinical Psychology Review(2010), doi:10.1016/j.cpr.2010.03

Zander, Rae (2014), Everyday Attraction. Topic: Doubt. Retrieved from: http://www.unity.fm/episode/EverydayAttraction_050214

APPRECIATION

To my editor, Marcia Craig; thanks for your ingenuity.
To my teachers: past, present, visible, and invincible;
    thanks for sharing.
Unto him who lives and dwells within me, whose life I
    call mine,
I owe this transcendent wisdom; thank you.

NOTES

1. THE AWAKENING

1. Philippians 4:13
2. Isaiah 41:10
3. Hebrew 13:5

2. UNLEASHING THE POWER OF THOUGHT

1. Psalm 82:6
2. Matthew 18:3
3. Genesis 13:15 (Paraphrased from the new living translation)

4. RELAX ... B-R-E-A-T-H-E ... LIFE IS GOOD

1. Luke 17:21.
2. Philippians 4:6.
3. Proverbs 23:25.
4. Jeremiah 29:11
5. Matthew 6:27

6. A MESSAGE FOR NEW IMMIGRANTS: IT'S ALRIGHT AND IT'S ALL GOOD

1. Psalm 30:5

7. THE POWER OF BEAUTY CONSCIOUSNESS: WOMAN, YOU ARE BEAUTIFUL

1. Psalm 139:14.

8. LET YOUR PASSION LEAD YOU TO SUCCESS

1. From *The Ladder of St. Augustine*, by Henry Wadsworth Longfellow.

9. THE CHARGE

1. 1 John 4:17
2. Matthew 19:26
3. Psalm 82:6
4. Psalm 82:6-7
5. Romans 8: 37

10. BE PATIENT...THE BEST WILL APPEAR

1. Romans 5:3-5.
2. Hebrews 13:5.
3. Ephesians 3:20.

17. PRELUDE: THE SUPERHUMAN WITHIN THE HUMAN

1. John Chapter 10 : 30 (King James Version)
2. 1 John Chapter 4 : 13 (King James Version)
3. 1 John Chapter 4 : 17 (Amplified Bible)

18. FORGIVENESS

1. Paraphrased - Luke 6:38b (King James Version)
2. 1 John 4:17 (Amplified Bible)
3. Matthew 4:10
4. Romans 12: 17 (King James Version)
5. Philippians 4:6 (New King James Version)

19. GRATITUDE

1. 1 Thessalonians 5 : 18
2. Romans 8:28 (King James Version)

20. AFFIRMATION

1. Hebrews 11 : 1 (King James Version)
2. Genesis 13 : 15 (King James Version)
3. 1 John 4 : 4 (King James Version)
4. Paraphrased - Isaiah 30:20 - 21 (King James Version)
5. Isaiah 46:11 (King James Version)

22. UNCONDITIONAL LOVE

1. Matthew 5: 44.

23. WHAT YOU GIVE, YOU RECEIVE

1. Romans 8:19
2. Ephesians 2 : 8

24. LIVING ABOVE FEAR

1. Romans 8:7 (King James Version)
2. Psalm 82: 6 (King James Version)
3. Philippians 4:6–8 (King James Version)

25. FIND YOUR HAPPY PLACE

1. Proverbs 4:23 (King James Version)
2. 1 Corinthians 9:27 (king James Version)
3. Matthew 6:33 (King James Version)
4. Isaiah 30:15 (King James Version)
5. Luke 17:21 (King James Version)

26. DIVINE FUSION

1. Psalm 82:6 (King James Version)
2. 1 Corinthians 6:19 (King James Bible)
3. John 4:21 (King James Bible)

27. FAITH AND GRACE

1. John 14 : 10
2. Ezekiel 21 : 27
3. Hebrews 13:5
4. Surah Al-Jumu'ah (62:11) – Al-Qur'an al-Kareem
5. Isaiah 46 : 11

Made in the USA
Middletown, DE
13 October 2021